THE ANCIENT ART OF
SELLING (OR BUYING) CARS

THE ANCIENT ART OF SELLING (OR BUYING) CARS

A 'CAR'EER GUIDE TO SUCCESS IN THE HORSE-TRADING INDUSTRY'S ANCESTOR (OR) HOW TO ALWAYS MAKE THE BEST CAR DEAL!

Roc Leatherbury

To order additional copies of this book, contact:
Xlibris Corporation
1-888-795-4274
www.Xlibris.com
Orders@Xlibris.com
25375

CONTENTS

PREFACE

"Advice is needed by many.
It is also heeded by too few.
But
Too much advice is neither heeded
Nor needed."

I certainly hope to abide by my own direction in the pages here to come. Furthermore, I hope to impress upon you the very lack of a seriousness demeanor we sometimes burden ourselves with in the pursuit of being ahead. Understand; I am not here to preach to you. Let's just say there's a tune for every band. We all have our various strengths and weaknesses. Use them both to the best of your abilities: your strengths are there to be honed even further and your weaknesses are there to serve as motivation to be merged unto your strengths.

Sounds like preaching to me. I'll move on.

Although the body of this writing is aimed toward the sales and related career in the automotive industry, the overall concept of the sales and executions of such may be related to virtually any other concepts of exchange-whether it is in furniture, real estate, banking, produce or whoopee cushions. It even could apply to personal relationships, at times. I try to make the point that we all have a degree of innate salesmanship in our beings and attempt to give enough information and examples for you to decide just how much is in *your* soul. Are sales for you? If so, which direction?

The whole concept of 'give and take', aka 'sales', is *universal*. For instance, plug in the subject of your choice into the place of 'car' and 'auto' and you may be surprised at how well the substitution could work.

Just don't replace "car" with 'mother-in-law' when referring to its underbody!

I am not copping out on the car dudes and "dudettes", however. This is for, about and focused on *CARS!*

Presumably, you're reading this for one of several reasons. One, you may be interested in the pursuit of a career in the automobile industry. Two, the auto industry may be pursuing *you* daily in the way of TV ads, full page newspaper layouts promising "Unbelievable Blowout Events" and fast talking radio ads (that only super sonic hearing devices could possibly understand and decipher) and you want to understand how to deal with it all a little better.

Perhaps you're already in the car business and you just want to check out what another "burn out" is trying to peddle upon the gullible public.

Then again, maybe word got out that this book is "The must read beach book of the season!" *"Unforgettable ending!"* . . . Sally Suitee, LA Passion. *"Suspense at its very best!"* . . . John Dork, Dilly Daily. *"Roc has outdone his past works by a Mars shot!!"*. George W. (just a passionate reader: Roc).

Be aware I will at times come from left field in my statements and comments. I'm not competing with Luis Gonzalez (I'm a big Arizona Diamondbacks fan!) but am being loose with this since I feel if you're having fun you will take it all in a little easier.

I will also assume, rightly or wrongly, you are a reasonably informed being that realizes information is there to be had through the Internet, the libraries and a multitude of periodicals available to anyone with a twitch. This is not a testimonial to how great I happen to be and having you believe "you, too, can be like me." It's not even a testimonial of others. No, this is real but it's all about YOU! No smoke; no mirrors: just my collection of my mentors' and my experiences being handed down to those for the asking and reading.

All in all, I make the attempt to give a sincere understanding of the basics of car "salespersonship". (You will notice my attempts at being an astute and politically correct person throughout.) I will hopefully show how the buying and selling of vehicles are intertwined inasmuch as when one knows how to sell, one knows how to buy. The opposite, of course, will hold, as well. Any misgivings any of you potential buyers may have will hopefully go by the wayside and you won't be quite as paralyzed the next time you do your car shopping.

For you currently employed as a salesperson, rest assured this is not yet another "How to Make the Car Dude and Dudette Look Silly While You Save an Average of 'Eleventy Seven Dollars Per Deal: Guaranteed!'" book. Rather, this is a "Any Successful Business is Out to Make Money and Be There for the Next Round When Services are Needed Again" book. Whewwww!

Reasonable people expect and want reasonable dealings. The more one is informed, the easier any process can and should be. Anyone reading this can expect to understand basic procedures in the 'guts' of the dealership where it all happens. I stress the point that no reasonable person expects another to lose money for the favor of doing a deal with him. If you do, you're an idiot or have some very revealing photos someone else doesn't want seen.

I will make a meager attempt at humor: please don't be offended when I do. I am told (by intellectually inferiors, I am sure you would agree) once in a while, quote: "You get a kick out of you, don't you?"

Well, yea, I do. I enjoy life. I have loved the car business. Sick, I know, but true! Love it now! I enjoy the camaraderie; the customers, the scene in general. Now and again, the hours at work are suspect but hey, it's just like "Disney World" on the fun meter. Why complain when you're being paid to have so much fun?

So, I make my attempt at communicating here. When people understand how others are going about to reach a mutual agreement, the road is a smoother one and all parties can prosper even more greatly. Customer services indexes rise. Referrals are more frequent.

The deal is a good one and there is money in your pocket. Whether or not I'm speaking to buyer or seller is for you to decide. Or not. Doesn't matter.

What matters is for you to sell/buy cars, have fun, make money!

A Little Bit of Real History: some facts and tidbits

I want to present a little bit of feeling to you. I want you to understand the industry that is still in the making and will be ongoing for generations to come. With a little thought, it's mind-boggling how much of a sociological effect the automobile has had on all of us. Change promotes change. Yet so much, like human nature, remains predictable. Facts follow. You fill in the blanks with your own stories.

You don't have to be a car buff to appreciate how the automobile has had such a profound affect on society and particularly here in America. The way of life as we know it has been literally steered there by that four wheeled load of metal, rubber and plastic. The evolution of the automobile began essentially in Mesopotamia around 3500 B.C. when the first wheels were put on a cart. Around 3200 B.C. Sumerians made use of wheeled transportation: pretty much "man power" since the horse was believed to have been domesticated around 2000 B.C. to handle such dragging and hauling.

Through creativity and imagination, the auto as we know it evolved from the basic cart and carriage concepts of the earliest times. Leonardo da Vinci and Sir Isaac Newton were known to have sketched theoretical drawings of motorized carriages. As a matter of fact, the term "automobile" was said to have been created by a 14th century Italian painter and engineer by the name of Martini. Understandably, drinking and driving had very honest roots.

Martini created the new term by combining the Greek word 'auto', meaning 'self' with the Latin word 'mobils', meaning 'moving'.

For a further root definition, the term 'car' was believed to be Celtic in origin deriving from the word 'carrus', meaning wagon or cart.

The term 'automobile' remained in hiding until an unflattering article in 1897 by the New York Times proclaimed, "The new mechanical wagon with the awful name (automobile) has come to stay . . . ."

Up to that point, the automobile had gone through various developmental stages starting in 1769 with Nicolas Cugnot, a French inventor who developed a working "tractor" powered by an engine run by steam. He persuaded the French army to make use of his handy invention by having them use it to transport artillery. Traveling at 2 ½ M.P.H. and having to stop every ten to fifteen minutes to "build up steam", the French gendarmes soon gave up on it and went back to their tried and true methods of horse teams.

Not to be deterred, Monsieur Cugnot improved upon his model until in 1771 he drove into a stone wall. Historians, accepting his concept "steam tractor" as an early form of an automobile, consider him as such to be the inventor of the first auto. He also has the honor of being in the first known automobile accident.

In 1801, Richard Trevithick built the first road carriage powered by steam. His was the first known in Great Britain. Through improvements, variations of his model carried passengers about London from 1820 to around 1840. Later banned, these versions were replaced by the railroad as its development moved ahead. In Paris, however, steam powered road tractors pulled carriages about until around 1850. Jumping across the "Great Pond", the idea spurred manufacturers in the United States to build steam coaches from 1860 through around 1880.

Toward the beginning of the new century, there were around 100 U.S. plants that manufactured "steamers". The Stanley brothers, Francis and Freelan, made advancements to the point where their "Stanley Steamer", nicknamed "The Flying Teapot", raced in 1906 at Ormond Beach, Florida and was clocked doing 127.6 M.P.H.!

Along with the "steamers" were the electric vehicles. Relatively simple, they outsold all other types around the end of the 19th century. Soon to be overcome by the internal combustion engines, the "electrics" nonetheless numbered around 35,000 on U.S. roads in the year 1912. With bulky batteries that were slow to recharge, they were doomed to go the way of the future Edsel until the turn of the next century.

Generally credited with ushering in the age of modern automobiles are Gottlieb Daimler and Karl Benz of Germany. In

1885, Daimler invented the prototype of the modern gas powered engine. In 1886, he adapted a stagecoach to hold one of his engines and created his version of a power carriage.

In 1886, Karl Benz patented the first gas-fueled car. As history and success have shown, they joined together in a very lucrative partnership shortly thereafter.

In spite of the developments of Daimler and Benz's, the first manufacturers of the gasoline powered vehicle were in France: 'Panhard and Levassor' in 1889 and Peugot in 1891. They were able to operate successfully through the purchasing of patents of others, such as Daimler and Benz, and marketing the finished concepts.

In the United States, James and William Packard and Ransom Olds were among the first manufacturers of autos. By 1898, more had started in the automobile venture and made more than fifty manufacturers in the nation. Names included Walter Chrysler, Louis Chevrolet, Henry Ford, John and Horace Dodge, David Dunbar Buick and James Packard. The brothers Mack, Duesenberg and White were all influential. There were the Stanley brothers with their steamers, as mentioned. The Fischer brothers are famous even today for the advent of the production of closed auto bodies.

Literally and figuratively, bumpy roads were the norm during the infancy of the automobile in the U.S. Opponents of the "devilish contraptions" thought them loud, stinky and not at all dependable: hard to crank, quick to stall and getting stuck in the smallest of potholes were typical. They caused traffic jams by interfering with the tried and true horse-drawn carriages-that was when the horses weren't spooked outright and bolting in frenzy when "alarumed" by backfiring engines.

Autos were so unpopular that many jurisdictions outlawed them altogether. Boston and Chicago were two such areas. Where they *were* allowed, warnings were required when vehicles entered certain areas. Some areas required the firing of Roman candles to forewarn. Others required bells on the wheels.

On the books were laws allowing disabling of these four-wheeled scourges. Chains, wire and rope were used to prevent the driving through otherwise "safe" neighborhoods. Even bullets were allowed to shoot out engines and tires as long as "care" was taken not to shoot the drivers or passengers. Speed limits were limited to 2 or 3 MPH and all motorized vehicles were required to yield to horses. Small towns were known to use stop watches to enforce the speeds and became quite "creative" in their charges and accusations. In 1902, such actions prompted the forming of the American Automobile Association, a.k.a. the AAA as we recognize it even in the 21st century. They helped in fighting the abusive police action. Their bumper stickers today help to identify those slow drivers in the passing lane.

Understandably, the popularity of the auto was slow to catch on in the early years of production since the wealthy were of the few able to afford one. The average annual salary was roughly $500 per year for the average citizen. A typical car tipped the scales at $1,000 to $1,500, two or three times their annual income. Relate the similar ratio in buying a home in today's marketplace. That cost was usually for the 'basic' vehicle: an engine supported on four wheels with a body carried along. Bumpers, headlights and even carburetors were considered accessories! Engines were hand cranked with broken arms to show for their efforts-sometimes, even death came as a consequence.

Spare gasoline at a cost of 60 cents per gallon at the local drug store was carried along in cans. Cars had little power. People were deathly afraid of the gasoline fumes.(Maybe that one they got right.)

Progress was a little slow to come, but come it did. Safety being an issue, in 1914 Detroit was the first known city to use manual stop and go signs. In August of 1914, Cleveland was the first to install an electric traffic signal. In 1924, the National Conference on Street and Highway Safety commission was formed. The chairman of the commission doubled as the Secretary of Commerce for the United States of America: Mr. Herbert Hoover. This group authorized a commission to draft a uniform code of highway safety for all 48 states.

Leading to the necessity of more wide scale regulation was the automobile becoming more affordable for the common folk. In

Lansing, Michigan, Ransom Olds invented the basic concept of the assembly line and was the leading manufacturer of autos from 1901 to 1904.

Henry Ford, taking notice, had a number of models in competition prior to his improved conveyor belt based assembly line system debuting from 1913 to 1914. Staring in 1903, there was the Model A, a 2 cylinder, 8 HP vehicle that sold for $850. 1904 brought the Model B with a 4-cylinder engine that sold for $2,000. In 1906, the 6 cylinder, 40 HP Model K could reach 60 MPH and sold for $2,800. At the time, the Cadillac sold for $800. The Ford Motor Company lost money and subsequently pursued a new direction. Adapting to the marketplace, the Model T, adapted from the Model N, was bought to fruition. It had a 4-cylinder engine with 2 forward gears and reverse, to boot. It would get 30 MPG and become popular overnight. In 1908, 10,000 were built. 1912 produced 78,000 of the model.

Necessity being the mother of invention, Ford needed to keep up with demand and filled that need with the assembly system in use after 1914. By 1927, when the last "Tin Lizzy", as the Model T came to be known, rolled off of the assembly line, 15,007,003 had been produced!

Ford reigned supreme for about 18 years and caused the demise of quite a few manufacturers. Filling the vacuums in the auto market, other companies emerged. William C. Durant, having already bought out Buick Motor Co. in 1904, incorporated the General Motors Corporation in 1908. G.M.C. merged Buick, Cadillac, Oldsmobile and the Oakland (Pontiac) motor companies. In 1916, a division destined to be the corporate leader, Chevrolet built a 4-cylinder model that eventually passed Ford as the best selling car in America.

John and Horace Dodge became strong competitors in this "horseless" race. Autos started to be seen coast to coast.

Coinciding with the growth in the U.S., the auto came on mightily in the early part of the 20th century. There were a great number of names to deal with as to just what the contraption was. Of the names offered, my favorite would have been the "OruktorAmphibolos"! Maybe that's just me-the name just rolls off the tongue.

Of less creative versions than "OruktorAmphiblols" were names early media references included: Autobaine, Autokenet, AutoMotorHorse, Autometon, Buggyant, Diamote, Horseless Carriage (finally sounded familiar, huh?), Mocole, Motor Carriage, Motorig, Motor-Vique, Oleo Locomotive, Road Machine, Motor Wagons, Mr. Henry Ford's early 'Quadricycle' and of course, 'automobile'.

Settling on the moniker of automobile, makers of the vehicles turned their creative endeavors to making the names of the models distinctly unique. From names of states, animals, stars, mythological figures and just plain old numbers and letters models were named. Examples of names include: Ajax, Apollo, Ben Hur, Goethe, Pan, Atlas, Vulcan (Yea, Spock fans!), Minerva and Sphynx: mythological stuff.

Lion, Lynx, Wolverine, Silver Hawk, Rabbit, Mustang, Wasp, Whippet, Wildcat, Road Runner, Pinto, and Lark are examples of the animal inspired labels.

Continuing with our breathing brethren, there were Badgers, Beavers, Black Crows, Crows (of any shade, one would suppose), Honey Bees, Jack Rabbits and Kangaroos.

I forgot to mention 'Seven Little Buffaloes'. Must have had to be there to understand that one.

Our heavens were so honored with names of: Flying Cloud, Golden Rocket, Sunset, Star, Vega, Jetstar, Galaxie, Sun, Moon, Nova, Meteor, and Satellite, among others.

How would you like to be behind the wheel of a Maryland? Or a Pennsylvania? The states were honored with a few models named for them. We heard of Chrysler's New Yorker but what about the Carolina? California? Virginian, Michigan, Illinois, Indiana, Ohio, Oregon, and the Texan were all names used to appeal to "state-riatism", I guess.

For those of you steering your De Ville, know your car was named after the founder of Detroit, Michigan in the 1700's. You knew, of course, the name of Antoine de la Mothe Cadillac.

For those who doubt Sears has everything: the Sears/Roebuck catalog once had among its items a motor buggy "so safe a child could run it."

Time moved on. The 1930's brought on the "People's Car" in Germany by the name of Volkswagen that offered more compact and affordable vehicles. The 1940's, stalled by WW II, nonetheless brought the Tucker, a car well ahead of its time, in 1948. Though pressured out of existence with only 51 cars made, historians agree that Preston Tucker influenced the surviving manufacturers with many of his innovations such as independent four-wheeled suspension, padded dashboards and "pop out" windshields. The "Cyclops" headlight didn't quite make the cut.

The 1950's and 1960's saw the American public become enamored with a larger, more luxurious automobile with loads of automatic features. Chromed, smiling or grimaced, grills greeted us through on-coming traffic. Cadillac's were pink; tops were down. Gas-guzzlers were adored.

The 1970's and 1980's realized new players in town: the Japanese automakers. Responding to the gas and oil crisis of the times, the American public responded favorably to the energy efficient and affordable compact vehicles. Moving manufacturing to the United States, the Japanese have become a mainstay and have now made the re-naming of the "Big 3 Auto Makers" necessary.

With the increased competition, the public was awarded with more efficient manufacturing by the use of robotics, safety of vehicles has vastly improved and cost/income ratios have decreased. Compare three times or more cost of vehicle versus income in 1900 to one third or half at today's income and cost.

The future of the industry is exciting to ponder with the introduction of the 'hybrid' vehicles. Hybrids, powered by a combination of gasoline and electric, are just beginning to tease the public's interest. 40,000 of these vehicles sold in 2003 with a forecast of 100,000 being sold in 2004. The vehicles offer reduced emissions and increased fuel efficiency without sacrificing performance and comfort.

The crossover has even begun with pickup trucks and sports utility vehicles coming out with their versions of hybrids. Having a past history of being used only for metro use, the hybrid is becoming one of everyday use for short trips or long distance driving.

By 2010 to 2020, it is predicted we will be utilizing vehicles powered by hydrogen fuel cells. Through the use of clean fuel, emissions will be zero with the "exhaust" literally being water so pure it could be drinkable straight from the tailpipe!

Such a short time to have come such a long way. Think of the influences we've experienced by way of the automobile and how it may yet have its spin on what's to come.

Think of the 1920's and the Model T that a farmer could mount a set of tractor wheels to when the field needed to be plowed. When he was done, a belt could be run from its jacked-up rear end set up to power the blade of the saw mill. Additionally, it powered pumps, generators, ground feed, shred grain, churned the butter, ground the meat and sheared the sheep. Neat! When the snow fell, a special undercarriage was developed for the Model T that came in handy for the northern climes. It was attached to the body so the front wheels could then be moved to the rear. With runners attached to the front axle, a "snowmobile" was created that was workable as well as fun.

Recall the drives through the country while being entertained by the famous Burma Shave jingles. Look how the gas stations turned into service stations, which grew into tourist's stops. Restaurants, hotels and playgrounds were born to accommodate the users of the automobile.

In California, the year of 1924, the name 'hotel' was combined with the word 'motor' to become the first ever 'motel'.

People grew to drive and be self-sufficient. Train schedules were no longer important. Buses could be avoided.

Once a month trips from the country to the city for supplies could be made daily, if wanted. Seeing that, people moved to the rural areas to escape the hustle and bustle of the city. Courtships covered hugely greater grounds. Some say the American breed is even improved by extending the mating areas. I am sure we all know people to prove that statement as a false one.

Of course, after the great moves to get out of the city, people still wanted the conveniences of the city so trade prospered with the development of the suburbs. The city came to them. Slightly more residential, the city came to the country. The automobile had helped to create a real estate revolution.

In Florida, curb services were established using bellhops. After all, who wants to leave the car? Food was served directly from grill to your window.

The government had curbside mailboxes installed.

Drive-In movies came into being. Necking was encouraged. More babies born. No kidding.

We can stay in our car to pick up prescriptions, buy liquor, drop off dry cleaning, eat, get married in or go to worship in. There are even places that provide drive-through funeral parlors!

There are about 130,000,000 passenger vehicles on this country's roads with another 40,000,000 types of vehicles to share them with. America owns 40% of all of the motor vehicles in the world!

Consider that amount when you take into account the population of Europe combined exceeds our own by 40,000,000! I don't think any can count the amount of Asians with respect to their vehicles.

Four of every ten Americans own two or more vehicles.

The American love for the automobile being what it is, Will Rogers once stated, "Americans would be the first people to go to the poor house in an automobile."

We are what we are. Face it: it is one of the greatest influences we have experienced in recent memory.

We ain't done yet, either.

It may just be you that puts a few spins on its future . . . .

Enjoy the book. Hope it helped whether you're pitching or catching.

. . . Even if you're playing in left field.

Roc

CHAPTER 1

SELLING (& BUYING) . . . CARS . . . PERHAPS?

It was a dark and stormy night . . . OK! . . . I'll stop with the dribble. But frankly, that was maybe the best way to start. You see, so many DO feel just that way when stepping onto a car lot. Polyester suits . . . gold chains . . . stogies emitted from orifices (THAT scares me!) . . . vultures ALL! . . . just waiting in clusters to descend upon fresh roadkill that just prior to pending evisceration had self-ejected from the security and safety of home, office or car. Pending doom; insight to the Armageddon fills body and soul, displacing bodily fluids to make way for its immense bulk. Fear is all encompassing. Thought patterns go awry. Self-doubt is overwhelming. Take me home, Elizabeth . . . I'm comin' to join ya, Honey! This is the Big One!

And THAT, my friends, is just from the point of view of the newly appointed car salesperson (a.k.a. "greenpea" in car lingo). Imagine, if you will (I Hate when people use "If you will" but it really works here. I promise not to use it again!), what the customer must feel! Just take those feelings to the Nth degree. It's frightening! Feelings of insecurity abound. Should I or shouldn't I? Can I or can't I? Will they or won't they? (If I could, would you . . . ?) . . . .

So, what has to happen for all of us to avoid this unnecessary trepidation? Knowledge? Insight? Experience? Aaahh . . . enlightenment! Key word, there. Light. As in enLIGHTenment. To see the light. To feel it. To Read about it. There ya go! You're already on the right track. And I hope you'll purchase my home improvement periodical on "Track Lighting" when I write that. But I digress.

Now, what does one do to gain this enlightenment? I posed this very question to myself several years ago upon moving to the self-appointed Car Capital of the World. That would be Phoenix. As in Arizona. As in the U.S. of the A. Dealerships abound: domestics, imports . . . Huge and huger . . . Number ones and number two's . . . Competition runs on and on. It's rampant and ruthless. And it does attract the best of the best in the business.

Some will ask, "What makes Phoenix, Arizona, the car capital of the U.S.?" Well, it is climate friendly. We all accept that even in 120 degrees in the shade it is a 'dry heat'. Yea, and so is a nuclear blast. Consequently, no salt or cinders are used on the streets and highways. No ocean-born salt is present in the air. Cars do last.

There are no cars that need snow 'broomed' off ("The car on the lot is just like the one you liked in the showroom, only different and covered with that white stuff!")

Retirement communities are ubiquitous. Industry is attracted. Sky Harbor Airport offers non-stop to London (for those nostalgic folks missing gloomy, foggy days).

Phoenix is just a few hours drive to coastal vacation spots (even if San Diego's body of water is on the wrong side . . . I'm a native Marylander, so *that's* weird).

Folks, the place is daggone-near recession proof. People keep coming and coming. And they keep buying cars: every year's sales' record seems made to be broken! In winter, Canucks arrive, eh? The Midwest is amply represented. A few strays like me settle here from the east. And the Californians who want to own waterfront in the future re-establish their nifty BMW's in garages housed in "Nostrodamus Estates".

The Cactus League is a huge draw in the area with more attendance records annually. The unbelievably successful Arizona Diamondbacks call this home for all of you wishing to participate in observing an already strong rivalry in the National League West.

All in all, perhaps the biggest draw to the area is to enjoy what new marketing strategies Bill Bidwell will employ with his 'O' so successful sports empire.

These are perhaps some of the reasons the Phoenix area does so well in the car industry, but the point is, it really is happening here. And happening big time.

After years of "being on the other side", I decided to get involved and figure out the good, the bad and the ugly of the automobile profession. Hell, it was for selfish reasons. I wanted to know; I wanted to make some money; I wanted to write a book about my experiences therein; I might even want to buy another vehicle some day and this would help me to know how.

And I could! I had the time and the motivation.

Now, a few years later, I tell a tale. My mentors have been among the best: sales people, managers, instructors, manufacturing reps, and of course, you and I, and thousands like us, who are also known as the customer.

The words herein are not meant to be taken literally as the one and only way to do things; as a matter of fact, part of what will be suggested is that we all have our own unique style and methods of successfully accomplishing our goals and objectives. Additionally, you may notice a slight hint of irreverence and frivolity . . . that, my friends, just happens to be the only way I'll even attempt to write what would otherwise be a dry, boring, and perhaps sanctimonious piece of diatribe.

In learning this business as the student, I also developed into what some even considered a more than adequate "mentor" in my own rights. Perhaps their qualifications as judges remains somewhat tainted, but my ego was stroked enough to at least write this book. The writing won't be a dream, but nor will it be dry, either.

For those of you considering a career in the automotive industry, I hope this work will help you to make the right selection as to whether it's for you or not.

For those of you already in the business here's wishing you perhaps even greater success with help from an outsider looking inside out.

For those of you buying, well, I wish you a GREAT deal! Aren't they all?

CHAPTER 2

SOCIOLOGICAL FOUNDATION:

THE BEGINNING

(A.k.a. the mercenary approach to Darwinism)

No attempt will be made to undergo any anthropological trek nor will I try to make the car buying and selling issues subject to psychological dissection. What I will strive to have understood is that the issue of "the deal" is not a difficult process to arrive at, after all. Although there will be those sales purists who consider the following story to be irrelevant, it's just an amusing and exaggerated tale of a trek of progressions in the pursuit of a process.

In fact, I believe the process to be so absolutely natural that to understand the workings, assumptions, goals and objections is merely to continue a cycle that not only have each of us practiced since birth, but in fact has been an integral by-product of thousands of generations of mankind preceding us.

We are from what we've evolved. We practice much of which we've been preached. Something goes in, a by-product is produced.

We ARE that by-product. We all want. We all have desires . . . dreams . . . hopes and expectations.

Generations back and generations hence, the same words can be spoken with truth and conviction. We are a species that have been subjected to satisfying three basic needs: Comfort, Love and Justice.

No matter what your physical, emotional or mercenary cravings and needs may be, all can be lumped into these three broad categories. And again, it's always been that way, and I guess until the cockroaches take over, it always will be.

One would then suppose that the most natural means of creating anything of substance would to in some way address the satisfying of these three basic drives:

Comfort.

Love.

Justice.

Piece of cake!

History Lesson

Back when the mighty mammoth roamed the edges of receding glaciers, transportation was pretty much in its rawest form. Org knew where his fueling stations may be by experience: which bulbs and roots to feast upon, where game happened to be frequenting, and of course, reliance upon his mate Tumba's special insight of knowing where rest stops were located.

A direct correlation existed between distance traveled and the thickness of foot callous. Hieroglyphics have long supported the theory that Mr. Goodyear's ancestors were indeed among the first of humanity to study the effects of tread wear. Instead of measuring transportation efficiency as miles per gallon, miles to the blister, as it were (you probably guessed I hated "as it were", too. Not to be used again!), happened to be the benchmark by which man and woman's worthiness was measured. The ability to travel long distances by the most efficient means possible was, even then, a highly regarded asset.

Of those in possession of this highly regarded asset, Org stood apart from the madding crowd. An exemplary specimen, he was stately for his time. His adornments were many; his accomplishments legendary, hunting skills unparalleled and his hands were big. How he and Tumba came to pass as partners is an exceptional tale of pre-recorded history.

The story that has been passed down through countless generations is that Org was renowned for his ability to cover vast stretches of land: he was first to find game, shelter and, on his good days, was able to secure a seat at the fifty bones line during the annual 'Super Kick the Head Bowl'. The latter supposition, however, is merely rumored.

Org was the finest at defending what was rightfully his. His humble cave, his various collections of tools, weapons and a primitive golf green were certainly secure. Org was "The Man". He was the latest and most 'state of the art' Cro-Magnon Motors had to offer! Cutting edge stuff! He was the model they All wanted!

But Tumba had wanted him the most. It is believed by many literary scholars that their meeting happened to be the Bard's inspiration in his creation of 'Romeo and Juliet'.

As the story (understandably, this will now be referred to as 'Herstory') goes, Tumba was no slouch in her own right. She was considered the most 'avant-garde' model of her time. She came standard in leather, self-designed and hand stitched using only the finest Corinthian Mammal. Her 'miles per blister' ratio approached that of Org's. She was self-cleaning and had the instinctive edge in making a cave a home. Her snake sushi was to die for!

And Tumba knew she just had to have the Org! Realize, fellow herstorians, this was not an impulsive gesture. Tumba did not wake up one morning and go immediately to Cro-Magnon Motors and just select what they had to offer. Au contraire! She thought and pondered, she cast out ideas, she thought of new prerequisites. The Great Fire of the Sky rose high and lowered itself many times while Tumba pontificated.

And a few moons passed.

———————————

Getting back to 'History', Org had decided that he, too, needed to expose himself to a greater and larger market. History did not clarify as to what the definition of 'expose' was. What was clear is that Org had known that he couldn't maximize his profit by merely touting his wares to the Bebakka twins or their 'innerbred' cousin, Tuhya. And although Gottagoa had certain allures that stirred certain ingredients in even the great Org, she could never be counted on to stay around long enough to completely comprehend if some form of transaction could be mutually beneficial.

Org was perplexed. How to find more opportunities was a troubling issue. So Org traveled to the highest precipice around and fasted three days and nights. He slumbered, chilly and hardened as he was to the rocky platform overhanging the great expanse of the uncharted plains.

He was barely aware of the pending storm front approaching when a bolt of lightning struck a nearby boulder, shattering and scattering it into countless shards of minuscule projectiles. Pain and revelation seemed to be co-existent, as these miniature missiles struck him in the cranial area, giving us the first recorded proof of a 'Brainstorm'. (Archaeologists of the nineteenth century uncovered multiple stone tablets in a 63 square mile radius exploiting Org's experience and prowess).

Of course, as I guess you now realize, Org's intent was to get his product out to more tribes. Let the people know he was good . . . he was available . . . and he was a bargain to be had! Painstakingly, he created many stone tablets that were dropped at watering holes, cave entrances, trail crossings . . . he even carved his extraordinary offer on the back side of trees where many were known to frequent when first awakening!

In what seemed to be no time at all, The Org was known by all! It had been a great deal of labor expended, but now Org was on the map. Had he only known Tumba already, a great deal of effort could have been avoided. But then, Org knew her only in his fantasies so his commitment was now to meet the material girl of his dreams. Did she exist, though? And, more importantly, would she need and want an 'Org'?

———————

Tumba had indeed decided that she did need an Org-like companion. She had "Ben Franklin'd" herself, studying the pro's and con's of such a commitment. But questions remained: *Could she afford an Org? . . . How long would an Org last? . . . .*

What would her friends think? . . . Would she regret her decision? . . . .

What few have recognized in herstory is that Tumba had had a relationship with a fellow sapien, but he was not of the normal Homo style. His vision was cracking, his body was dinged and scarred, and he leaked a great deal of gas! He was actually getting to be a danger to be around! He was often difficult to get started, and once he did get going, she prayed she could get him stopped! He no longer traveled to get her the Corinthian Mammal so in demand by her fellow tribes-people and she had debts to honor.

As luck would have it (at least that's what She thought), Tumba was picking berries near a trail crossing in front of a friend's cave near the local watering hole when nature called. Although she had tripped over those daggone stone tablets, she hadn't taken the time to truly study them, preoccupied as she was in thought. Finally relaxing, and in a more comfortable state of mind, Tumba happened to glance at a message that was literally in front of her face. It was the 'Org'! What she knew she needed but had really kept suppressed. "This is it!" she exclaimed. And Tumba proceeded to confront her sapien mate of the unusual Homo variety.

Unfortunately, Tumba found that the little worth that her mate may have brought forth was history. An unauthorized female had in fact jump-started him and his remains were to be pulled from a rocky ravine. The female said that she had, in fact, tried to stop him, but all attempts to do so had failed. Conjecture is that the remains of his bones were salvaged and later utilized as markers at 'Kick the Head' contests, but Tumba's compensation was minimal at best. No recorded proof of any compensation exists outside of a one game ticket for a perch located in the end zone, however. Little has been handed down concerning the relationship of Tumba and the unauthorized female. There were probably few who cared.

Tumba was a little disappointed, but she had at least gotten her money's worth out of him during his more productive years. The pity was that his production ended as parts were salvaged to be used as bone markers for the contests. She was in need of a new "vehicle". Such a shame . . . really! But there was that ad about the 'Org-dude' she had seen scattered about. A little disappointment quickly turned to excitement.

So . . . on to see about the 'Org'. It looked to be an OK deal. It was time to see about getting up close and personal and check this stuff out!

Tumba had copied the 'Org' site given on the tree onto a compact disk (a small, thin egg-shaped piece of shale) and proceeded across the uncharted plains in search of her great deal. Although the directions given were in a rather circuitous design, she traveled on, bringing forth strength and stamina by recalling the words of her elders: "A journey of 63 miles begins with one step." So on she trucked.

Tumba had also recalled her elders saying of ". . . getting there is half the fun", so she did, in fact, dawdle just a mite. She had decided that the painted palm leaves and coconuts dangling by the trail sides in various camps were just too curious to pass by. Certainly, she thought, there must be something very special going on here.

Oh, what glorious displays! Org-like creatures were displayed at their finest! Men were lined up shoulder to shoulder. Some were standing on large boulders placed at trailside. Their bodies shined, glistening even, as though perhaps applications of mammal lard had been placed to accentuate every subtle line and curve. Some had limbs outstretched with some of those painted coconuts dangling from them! Others stood motionless with mouths gaping ajar!

Yes! Glorious displays, all! Tumba really had to take pause and reflect: "Perhaps I could save some traveling. Maybe I could get an Org-like deal here. I wonder?" . . . .

Some of these specimens came with promises of free feedings for the first two moons. Others were attired in plant-like coverings while still others were covered in the Corinthian Mammal Tumba had such affection for. There was even one that bellowed such harmonious song that Tumba seemed to be enveloped by reverberating chords of music!

But none seemed to be quite the Org-like model that she had envisioned.

She was offered alternatives. Offers of free flint stones were suggested. A sling was offered to be thrown in as good measure. Rocks for the sling . . . A spear came into the picture . . . A stick with a thin vine attached to the end was laid on the table. Dangling from the end of the vine was a curved bone. This new device was reputed to be the latest in getting fish by getting the curved bone into the fish's mouth. This was getting tempting! Tumba was even offered a bowl of worms to place on the curved bone to attract the fish!

Tumba was weakening! This was all getting to be too much! All of these 'Org-dudes' were all right, but none were *Just* right. But the perquisites were getting way too tempting.

She was just about done. Tumba had been "what iffed", "if I could'd", "wouldn't you'd", . . . ad infinitum . . . .

So, she thought she'd maybe give it a try. Just a try.

And she was informed that it would have to be seen if she, in fact, qualified.

Standards in the days of Org and Tumba were established by the amount of lizards and reptiles that one had contributed to the tribal well-being. You see, the succulent meat was a delicacy, the bones were favored for this new fish catching contraption, the heads were added to make an otherwise bland gumbo grand indeed, and the feet were dried and hardened to be adorned on various extremities of the body denoting tribal rank. The skins, however, were the most prized of all. The skins, after all, were the sole source of clothing for the tribal Wizers of the time. By law and tradition, only the Wizers were allowed to sport such extravagant threads and others could only don said threads at the penalty of banishment for a first time offender and death at the second indiscretion. (Note: no deaths for this offense were ever recorded due to the fact no one ever heard from the "banishees" again).

So, questions were asked of Tumba. Where was her cave . . . How long had she been there . . . How could she be reached . . . Had she had a mate before . . . .

Question after question—But the singularly most important question remained: How many reptiles did she work on in a month? This answer was placed under the heading of "Total Reptiles Worked", or commonly shortened at the time to TRW.

Tumba brought smiles to all around! After all, she was legendary in her tribal grounds for her consistency in working the lizards and reptiles! Heads, claws, skins and fins: she was The Best! This tribe had never seen a better accounting of a TRW! (Note: a.k.a. in the future as 'Evolutionary Extractions Performed' and shortened to 'EXP'.)

Everything seemed to going nicely. Tumba was going to take the Corinthian-clad specimen, glistening as he was. A bright yellow coconut bobbed merrily from the thong wrapped around his skull. She twitched his nose and a melodious tune sprang forth. All was right in the world.

But suddenly Tumba realized she hadn't examined one of the most important features of all: the soles of his feet!

It now occurred to her that all of these specimens were standing on and in pods of "mammal pie", surreptitiously showcasing their products. *Something was just Not right!*

Rearing her leg back, Tumba let forth with a kick to the ankle area of her "Org-dude". The "Org-dude" then proceeded to bellow and rage while lifting his foot and leg wholly from the 'pie'. Tumba then helped with his momentum by lifting under his calf and propelling him to the ground. What a sight! "Org-dude" was face-down in a mammal pie, Tumba astride his backside while twisting his legs to the heavens, all the while trying to scrape previous mammal meals from the bottom of his feet. Others were encircled around the melee, screaming disclaimers and enticements while still maintaining a smile!

"Just as I thought!" screamed Tumba. "No pad! No good! No deal!"

With an attempt to control Tumba's emotions just a little, reminders of the flint, the spear, the free meals, and the fish-catching contraption were all suggested. Even offers of putting the worms on the curved bone were suggested.

And even though Tumba was a little pacified, she still felt the deal was of much less merit with so little tread wear remaining on the "Org-dude". "Why should I take this less than perfect specimen?", she demanded. "It's really less than I had originally bargained for!"

She was asked what other offer could be entertained.

"I see no other offer that would interest me. Nothing!"

Then she was asked if she would consider the deal if someone would even be willing to put the worms on the curved bone yet again. And yet even another time!

"No!" she exclaimed, "I'll not do this deal if you bait my bone! Even if you re-bait it! Or offer a double re-bait!"

With that statement, much to the chagrin of those remaining, Tumba referred to her compact disk and proceeded to continue on in the direction first started: all signs led to Org.

———

It has been said that in the time of Org and Tumba that much reverence was paid to "The God of the Seventh Day". Knowing that even a god needed rest, activities were limited to paying homage to their deity and great feasts were often observed. Aside from the preparation of the meals, the only acceptable work related activity was in the design and creating of the Wizer's garments. The Wizer's attendants made certain all adhered strictly to 'God's' word.

With all due respect to Wizer's Day, as it was called, Wizer's Eve was heralded as a day filled with contests, trade, boar rides and reptile juggling exhibits. As Tumba continued on her trek to Org, distractions were many as she passed through various clan lands since it was, indeed, Wizer's Eve.

Had it not been for her previous bad experience with the 'Org-dude' lot, Tumba may have been more inclined to take a little time to examine the offers of the many showcaves along the way. Again, painted coconuts and palm leaves were displayed, accompanied by gap-toothed smiles with promises of being the best. Curiously, different clan lands offered different assortments of 'Org-dudes' owing, Tumba supposed, to the different demands of the immediate environment of said clan. One showcave had the newest 'Work-Org' which was hugely broad of chest, complete with bulging biceps and a distinguishing flat skull. Rock and boulder displacement was apparently this dude's specialty.

At another showcave, Tumba spotted a most novel concept: the 'Compact-Org'.

Standing a little over four feet tall, this model's apparent worth was in the invasion of animal burrows, collecting not only fresh game, but eggs and the heralded lizards as well. In addition, the 'Compact-Org' used little fuel to operate and took very little space to park in the cave. One was even a mute, with quiet operation a distinct advantage.

Clan-land after clan-land, Tumba took in all of the sights and offers of Wizer's Eve. There were stands on the trail with displays of shells and trinkets, hides and tools, Elvis-Org portraits, and even a walk-in stand featuring corn lizard on a stick! Clans people stood around them all, bartering with what they had to offer. Commonly, Elvis-Org portraits were exchanged for the equivalent of eight flint stones, but sometimes customers walked away with this treasure for as little as three stones. Others, caught up in the emotion of Wizer's Eve, lightened their load by as many as thirteen stones, two lizards on sticks, and gave up a thorough session of skull-lice removal to gaze daily upon this glimmering Stone-N-Roll idol.

Tumba overtook many 'Org-dudes', encumbered as they were with mistresses and various passengers mounted upon their bodies. Some of the multi-purpose 'Orgs' even had a passenger astride each shoulder with a third strapped to an optional rear seat. Tumba reflected on how even great 'Org-dudes' such as she was seeing and passing up were of great use, even slowed as they were by their loads.

Progress was slowed at a major intersection where trail repair crews were affecting path repairs. Tumba noted with interest how a one-legged 'Org-dude' was utilized in the compacting of the surface. While simultaneously being fed coffee beans and tickled in the ribs with a dodo bird feather, men held him by each arm while his leg spasmodically hammered the dirt and stones into a hard and firm pavement. She gazed on in fascination once this 'Org-dude' finally tired of tamping, spent and exhausted. His handlers then proceeded to drag him back up-trail where the surface had been completed, dipped his foot into a vat filled with an orange dye, and dragged him, foot "in toe", down the center of the trail, leaving a solid orange line in their wake. Once the 'Org-dude' showed signs of revival, they repeated their trip up-trail, dipped his foot once again into the vat, fed him even more coffee beans to chew, and dragged him beside the previously laid line. With his leg again "spazzing out", dashed, orange markers on the trail gave testament to the fact that this was, indeed, a really multi-talented 'Org-dude'. Nonetheless, though very intrigued, Tumba felt she had best move on.

After detouring the construction site, she took notice of a kick the head contest taking place. On the outskirts of the event she took notice of a score or more 'Org-dudes' filed front to back. All wore yellow hides with black markings and spoke a language that even she had trouble understanding. Upon inquiring, Tumba found that these 'Org-dudes' were waiting for the finish of the event to transport skull groupies, as they were called, to their requested destination. The fee was bartered; tips were optional but mandatory.

Tumba had become so enlightened on this journey! She had no idea of the various array and uses of the 'Org-dudes'. There were so many styles, looks, applications, and of course, the equipment varied greatly.

However, the message she had seen not only on the tree but on the multitude of tablets throughout the great land had convinced Tumba that she would make no move until she checked out this 'Org'!

And on Tumba trucked.

All the while that Tumba had been experiencing her odyssey through the plains, Org had been cranking up on his new-found marketing strategies. In addition to his tablets and tree carving procedures, he had been doing a little hole to hole selling at the caves as well. Since his distribution of "product literature" had required him to travel great distances, and also because of his excitement at the prospect of realizing the girl of his dreams, preoccupation had clouded his sense of direction just a little.

Org was at most times very aware of his whereabouts as he was greatly experienced in hunting expeditions and in his exploration of lands to the north and west. However, this trek had taken him to heretofore alien territories which were not only to the south and east, but after the uncharted plains had taken him into valleys surrounded on all sides by towering mountains. Where he had normally traveled, the heavens were his guide. It had been overcast in this new place for days now. When it had been cloudy or rainy in his past travels, he'd use the moss covered side of the trees to take a reading. All of the trees in this strange land were encircled by moss. When all else had failed, Org had a terrific sense of smell and could distinguish his bearings detecting sources in the wind currents. Besides the birds and primates skittering in the treetops, a leaf hadn't so much as twitched since entering this valley days ago. His terrific smelling unit was of little use under these conditions.

A little humbled, but nonetheless willing to make the best of the situation, Org had decided to test his "product" at the caves of this foreign place. He figured that, with a little subtlety, he could slip in a few questions as to his location, check out the neighborhood, and maybe, just maybe, chance upon the fantasy mate he'd been searching for.

He certainly did meet some strange folks! And brother, they weren't too friendly, either. He was demeaned, cussed, poked in the foot by sticks too many times to count, dogs had bitten him (he DID bite a few back, though!), and the females that he did happen to spy upon had been visually challenged. That is to say that Org's vision had been challenged when he glanced upon them.

The Bebakka twins were suddenly looking better and better. At least they promised something, if not exactly what Org had in mind.

He couldn't figure what was wrong with these people in this strange land. *Maybe it was this unseemly climate*, he thought. Traveling hole to hole, his smelling unit sure went into overtime at each cave. With no fire in the sky, Org supposed that smells had a way of lingering a little longer and stronger. Maybe it was no wonder that these people had such a funky disposition, after all.

The real downside to all of this rejection and dejection was, however, his lack of being able to discover where to set his sights to get the heck out of Dodge. Wandering aimlessly was not one of Org's favorite pastimes. In fact, this was something he now only discovered about himself since he'd never had the occasion to even consider its possibility. But wander he would, since he recalled the advice of his elders, ". . . a journey of 63 miles begins with one step."

Two days and nights had passed since Org had even set his looking units on another dude or dudette. It wasn't an altogether bad feeling, though. With his recent interactions only now settling to the rear of his cranium, he'd come to feel more like the real Org he had always been: secure, strong-strong of both hoof and mouth, . . . strong of back . . . strong of front . . . Strong! Yes! As to where he was, he didn't know yet, but he'd fed well and the skies appeared to be lightening up ever so slowly. Hope was returning. He'd make it home to his own showcave and a variety of females would be there awaiting his return. Excitement was trickling into his soul once again. He just hoped that he was traveling in the right direction, though. That would really be a big help. Just in case, he decided to make camp for the night next to a river bed. After all, he had this new fish catching contraption that he had absconded after a mutant cave dweller had unsuccessfully attempted to lash him with it. It sure is a good thing the dude had yelled, "Come back with my new, state of the art fish catching contraption complete with curved bone to place in mouth of fish after baiting with worm." Otherwise, Org may have thought it a tool to warm snake sushi with over the fire. Things may not be the best, but maybe, in the words of the elders, "every rain puff over the mountains does have a fire on its edges."

Org settled his goods within a bush, began a fire by the riverbank with his trusty flint stone, walked to a nearby tree at water's edge, slid himself down to a comfortable position, and lowered his curved bone into the water.

His last conscious thought was *"life just might be getting better, after all . . . ."*

Since departing the clan-lands to the south, Tumba had been doing a little cogitating on the subject of Org-dudes. The weather had been very unseemly, blanketing the terrain in a heavy fog, and although the directions she had acquired from the dudes in yellow hides with black markings had been more than adequate, the trip had been quite boring, indeed. The scenery had been unremarkable, since very little could be seen, so the trip had become a little boring. "To cogitate picks up the gait." Ah, the words of the elders comes through once again. Indeed, she had been making pretty good time in spite of the weather and although the sounds of a violent storm due north had caused her to detour in an easterly direction, the varieties and possible consequences of Org-dudes had been a source of amusement in her travels.

Realizing that the foothills were taking her to the edge of the plains, Tumba traveled even more in a nor'easterly direction, questing for the higher grounds which could perhaps give her better bearings and a drier walk, to boot.

"This Org had better be worth it", she said to herself, "If he isn't, I'll just continue with my Tumba's liberation movement."

Tumba certainly was finding herself with all of that cogitation taking her into previously unexplored realms of new ideas.

But she also thought about the give and take of having an Org. An Org could help supply her with mammal hides; an Org could help defend her cave; a Good Org could enable her to raise a family.

Of course, a Good Org would also tie her down with orgettes.

He may just lie around on Wizer's Eve at 'kick the head' contests.

He might even turn into a sapien not of the normal Homo variety.

She would probably have to cook and clean even more lizards and reptiles.

However, isn't it nice to have an Org to hold your hide open at the cave entrance? And ambiguously, isn't it nice to open your own hide at the cave entrance . . . or anywhere else, with the right Org?

Ah, to have him there when you wanted and needed him . . . .

Would he be there when I wanted and needed him? . . . .

"Oh, fear of loss", she was thinking. "Buyer's remorse and I haven't even bought, yet."

Give and take, touch and go, yin and yang, to and fro . . . Tumba's cogitating had taken her into really confusing grounds. And speaking of confusing grounds, she noticed she really had lost her way. All of this Org-thought had made her trip a little quicker, but quicker to where, she didn't know.

She had recalled talk of a river from the mountains that flowed into the plains. Since Tumba had seen nothing larger than a stream since departing, it certainly had to be ahead. And since the river traveled northwesterly, after finding it her quest would hopefully soon be over, her Orgdeal both behind and ahead at the same time.

"Yes", she mumbled, "This is turning into more of an Orgdeal than I had planned."

Tumba was tiring. Foot pads were tested, Corinthian Mammal soaked, cranial area hurting, she decided that this day was about done and looked for an area to make camp for the night. Although the footing in these higher grounds was firmer, finding dry tinder turned into an exercise in futility.

Her search carried her to a crest overlain with a myriad of vines and undergrowth. Burrowing through scant openings created by the area's game, Tumba was on the verge of collapsing when a familiar sound just barely tickled her hearing units. A small rush of cascading, tumbling noises, so unlike the death-like loneliness of fog, penetrated her senses, instilling newfound invigoration. "Could it be the river?", she croaked.

Pulling herself clear of the brambles and vines, Tumba descended the knoll, head tilted, willing her hopes to be true. "Where there's will, there's a way". Tumba thought she'd have to remember that to tell to the elders. Perhaps she'd earn the right to wear another lizard's claw with that revelation.

Indeed, that was the way! Not only was her descent covered with ease, but on this side of the hill the ground was much less soaked, allowing her even more optimism in regards to being able to produce fuel for her fire.

The sounds of the river grew in volume with every slip, slide and stride. The air was even a sound, a sight, an entity unto itself as the freshness seemingly permeated every one of her senses. Tumba could feel the river just ahead.

That's when a familiar odor hit her! Smoke! Could the storms have hit here? Did a fire spear strike a tree? Tumba had seen what damage fire spears had done to the forests in her own clan land. The elders even spoke of the times of the great past when the plains were not plains at all, but dense with magnificent towering trees. The gods may play with fire spears, but Tumba wanted no part of the playground.

Senses heightened, Tumba sought the refuge of the river she knew to be ever closer. Though weary and cold, she preferred safety and solace of the healing waters to the alternative of a god's version of 'Tumba on a stick'. After all of this effort, she was bound and determined to acquire her Org!

Her Org! Through all of her trepidation, her Org was foremost in her mind! At that moment, she knew she really must have him.

All of her doubts, though not entirely vanquished, were at least lessened immediately. She knew she had to save herself, if only to get the chance to see if this Org was the right way to go. Tumba was inspired!

And also perspired . . . Tumbas don't "sweat". And speaking of 'pires', that's exactly what Tumba saw when she first laid eyes on the river: a pyre, that is. At least a pyre is the first thought that came to mind. A magnificent, roaring blaze was situated beside the river bank. Circling the fire were moderately sized boulders to contain its wrath and giving the whole scene a somewhat ceremonial atmosphere.

But who started this fire . . . and where were they?

Org had been dreaming. In the dream, he had seen himself being pursued by a gorgeous, wisp like creature: a blur of long, golden hair trailed her movements as she flowed through the wooded trails. Her looking units were the color of the great waters, her skin bound with shiny, hide-like coverings. Clawed feet were adorning her hearing lobes: he couldn't tell if they were part of her or merely trinkets. This was a disturbing thought.

There was a grand, absolutely sparkling smile, though, that seem to vanquish any fear that he maybe should have had. A light surrounded her entire face that shaded any hint of what this creature looked like, but Org knew this had to be a sign of good fortune. Her hands outstretched, she continued her traipse, getting ever closer, while the light from her face grew stronger still. In her hands, Org noticed a small, circular shell that the light from her face seemed to be reflecting upon. The light kept getting brighter and brighter until it seemed to be turning colors and turning the shell into a spinning globe that in turn began to disperse bolts of fire, not unlike the fire spears that the gods were known to play with during the great storms.

Closer and closer she came, and with her the multi-colored bolts of fire. One bolt shot by his leg, barely missing. Another struck the bush he was standing near, setting it ablaze. Strangely, Org still felt no fear but rather, he was beginning to be aroused.

In a flash, millions of bolts came forth from the shell, striking him at once and surrounding him in a cell of rainbow colored strands, rendering him virtually immobile. Beads of sweat brushed against his confinement causing miniature, explosive sparks.

He remembered thinking in his dream, "how can I be moved, and not be moved at all?"

With this question, Org felt a familiar stirring in his lower regions. That was when the rainbow cell began to pull him over on his side. Where and what and who and when and how and why . . . . ?

Org quickened as he came to grips with where he was: lying on his side at the base of the tree. Clamped between his thighs was the fish catching contraption rocking back and forth, back and forth. Setting himself upright, Org shook the sleep from his eyes and peered over the river bank to see the curved bone at the end of his line attached to a piece of driftwood that was sloshing with the waves into the shoreline.

That was when he realized he was surrounded by smoke and noticed the source as being his own garments. As he was sleeping, the wind had shifted and blown Org's campfire sparks to seek refuge with their creator. His dream blended quickly into reality.

And the creator sought refuge with the waters of life as he quickly plunged feet first into the "first" river he could find.

Tumba had composed herself while surveying the scene below her position. Walking in unannounced was not what one would usually find in one's best interest when chancing upon the threshold of an unfamiliar camp; particularly one that had such a large fire with no tenders in the immediate area.

Finding comfort at the base of a large tree, she had settled behind a stand of shrubs and covered herself with a thick layer of leaves and needles. Both camouflaging and warming her, Tumba was patient to wait out the inhabitants below and determine whether friend or foe they be. Or if indeed it was a 'they'. Perhaps it was a him or a her.

Settled between the mountains, darkness was descending a little sooner than accustomed so the large fire was beginning to accent the immediate area a little more with a wavering casting of light. The boulders surrounding the 'pyre' seemed to taking on a distinct yellowish glow while actually seeming to pulsate as if they had a life of their own. Fixating on the boulders, Tumba seemed to notice pustules emanating from the boulders on the far side, bursting with distinct blubbering's and pops.

Within moments, Tumba detected a sweet, pungent odor in the air, reminding her of her thirst and hunger. Ever patient, she remained motionless, awaiting the answer to this puzzling scene before her. The air became sweeter still . . . and more enticing.

Tumba created a mental diversion to escape the unpleasantness of her thirst and hunger by keying in on what she imagined her Org to look like. He must be tall and firm, she thought. Quick of wit would certainly be a plus. An able hunter and good traveler were facts she had already assumed to be true after deciphering the tablets strewn about the countryside. She wondered what his culture was like and if he was allowed to be playful and silly at times. Was he a man to take charge of his mate? Probably . . . and she was sure he wouldn't be an abusive individual.

More and more Tumba thought about what was now "her" man. *"If only he's as real as I want him to be"*, she thought.

With more comfort than she thought possible in the given situation, Tumba realized she had fallen in love with a man she had yet to meet. Considering all that she had gone through, and with the question of what was yet to come, she also felt a little of what one of her descendants, Job, would feel thousands of years from now.

Tumba had left the sanctity of home. Her friends were long behind her, maybe never to be seen again. She was chasing an illusive dream of a man that may not even exist, lying in needles and bugs and bug doo-doo while being tempted by a mystical aroma created by who knows what or who. There is no justice in life sometimes . . . Well, talk about a mental diversion quickly leaving! It was just as well, since splashing was accompanied by crashing, banging and loud guffaws. Something, or someone, was sure making a racket, but Tumba was unable to see what or who it was. All of the brouhaha was happening just beyond the edge of the fire light but the oncoming melee was approaching in a hurry.

Tumba readied herself to be in a defensive, if not a retreating, position . . . slowly brushing nature's blanket from her body. Quietly, she unsheathed her blade and furtively moved to the side of the bush she had been behind. Willing her breathing and heart rate back into control, Tumba decided to chance a little closer view, slowly, ever so slowly, bringing one foot in front of the other, closer . . . closer . . . .

Wouldn't you know it, at that moment a whole covey of spotted owls happened to pick that moment to start hooting and screeching all around Tumba. On edge, she let out a whoop all of her own, probably making the spotted owls envious of her stellar performance. Damn, she hated those damned owls . . . they seemed to be everywhere!

"Who goes there . . . . ?" a voice boomed from around the fire. "Stand and be counted!" it roared.

With little to lose, only her life, which at this moment wasn't a whole lot of fun, Tumba decided on taking a spin on the wheel of fortune. Certainly, nothing was down pat at the moment, but maybe things would be all "White". (As in Vanna! OK-groannnn!)

Replacing her knife in its sheath, Tumba responded in as innocent a way as she thought possible. "Put down your weapons! I mean no harm, but if you do not cooperate, my forces will strike you down. You are surrounded!"

The very definition of hubris, Tumba walked down to the fire head held high, back straight, eyes narrowed to the source of the sound. "You need not fear me, but if you resist, you will sleep with the fishes! Hands behind your head and step into the light!", Tumba ordered.

As Tumba stopped at the edge of the camp, she wasn't prepared for the sight in front of her. She was totally startled!

For what was confronting her, she had no words to express. Two men, at least she thought they were men, had approached with their hands behind their heads, kneeled to the ground at the border of the fire, and started with prayers and litanies of the type she had never before heard. As strange as their tongues seemed, their appearance was even more bizarre.

One had the most flesh Tumba had ever seen enveloping a sapien, of any variety, in her life. His belly actually rolled and lapped over his knees and seemed to invite one to enter by continuing onto the ground in front of him in a step-like fashion. There were sporadic tufts of hair growths sprouting from his sides, front, and back. She knew of the large amount of hair on the back because the wind would whip it around, slashing at its master.

As if there wasn't enough to go around already, this fellow had three breasts, overlapping each other on their way down to the 'stair' belly. Tumba didn't know how many stones this giant weighed, but the quarry had certainly been emptied.

And his head! His head was not much larger than Tumba's fisted hand. And his looking units were where his hearing units were supposed to be! And he had but one hearing unit where his eating unit was normally located with two, yes two, smelling units immediately above. She didn't see his eating and talking unit, but her guess as to where was probably right.

The other was equally disturbing to behold, but in a diametrically opposed fashion. At first, Tumba thought she was observing an apparition as she took in the sight of a floating orb, bobbing to and fro, seemingly unsupported. As her looking units adjusted to the light, she realized with a start the orb was indeed held up by this wraith-like stick of a figure. The orb was this stick's head! "By the gods", she thought, "this one would have to run around in a waterfall just to get wet! If he were squatting to relieve himself, he'd have to worry about falling through his own waste unit and hanging himself."

With that ridiculous thought in mind, Tumba started to chuckle. And her chuckling grew. Soon, she was overcome with uncontrollable laughter, her stomach aching and all limbs losing control. Imagine this huge head being hanged by his waste unit! And this head where the eating unit was placed directly on top of the skull! If he didn't die of hanging, he certainly wouldn't die of thirst! At least during the rainy season. But eeewww, what torture the smelling units would be going through with all three of them placed around where the jaw line should be.

Gaining a little of her control back, she became a little more objective. What freaks of nature was she confronted with? They appeared to be harmless, yet how could one not be a little disconcerted when presented with such a scene? 'Skull' was hairless—totally— unless you counted the patch on each of his elbows.

Neither wore adornments of any nature, they were cowered with the slight suggestion of a strange female, no weapons seemed available . . . and then Tumba realized that they did have something in common: they were both totally yellow! Not in a jaundiced fashion, but good, old style, tulip on a stem, dandelion yellow! And the hair was lime green!

Now, that would create a challenge for a marketing campaign!, Tumba thought. *What a strange duo!* "Who are you men?", she asked.

At first, neither would speak. She could feel that the pair happened to be totally intimidated but their body language didn't give her a clue. Tumba could not speak their kind of body language, so it must have been her intuition.

"Again! Who are you men and what clan land are you from? And what are these strange, popping boulders you have placed about your fire?", she asked.

She thought she heard a response, but could not make out the words. It sure would be nice to be able to see the talking units when they were talking. "Turn so I can see your face. I mean, let me see your talking units when you speak."

Carefully, 'Blob' turned his apple-sized head almost all of the way around and, as Tumba suspected, his talking unit was on the back of his "cranium".

Not quite as carefully, 'Skull' tilted his head forward but with his obvious lack of ballast, quickly came crashing down on his face.

At least Tumba could now see his mouth when he spoke as it was on the top of his head. This whole scene certainly was unsettling, though. A huge mouth with a stick attached to it next to a quivering mass of yellow jelly supporting a lump of a head.

A voiced squeaked out. "We're the Lemon brothers", the 'Blob' wheezed. "My given name is Sally, but you can call me Al. My brother here's given name is Mos'ly, but you can call him Al, too. Since ain't nobody ever around us, when we hear "Al" called out, we knows somebody to be talking to us. Knows who say'd it, too. Al did!"

The 'Skull' boomed in response, "I'm Al!"

As strange as this scene was, Tumba felt a mite relaxed around this harmless couple of 'Al'. And strange they were. "Well, Al, would you mind letting me in on the little secret as to what these boulders are surrounding your fire? What are they . . . and why do they smell so tempting?"

Al looked at each other. Al decided to let Al explain. "Why, they's lemon, missy. Wrapped and stacked in green vines, they is. Tied together like that they look like boulders. They be marinatin' and stewin' in they's own juices. Looky here on the ground under 'em is where they be a placed upon be the shell o' the great giant river oyster. You see, Al and me, well, we knows how to catch the great oyster. Ain't for all to know, neither. If it wasn't for all your tribe around us an' such, were I to tell you the great oyster secret, well, Al an' me, we'd have to kill ya. An' that's a fact. So, I guess a good oyster secret's worth keepin", the 'Blob' explained.

"I still don't understand", Tumba replied, "what the shells do and besides, you do know, don't you, that when one knows something, it's a secret. When it's shared by two or more, it's just common knowledge."

With that sudden insight, Al looked at each other suspiciously.

Tumba noticed the tense moment, but after a spell, both noticeably relaxed. She guessed they forgot that they maybe shouldn't trust each other. These Lemons were a trip.

"Well, missy, I guess you didn't notice the drippin's in the shell. I'm guessin' that's what they be for, don't you know! You see, we trap the great giant river oyster so's we can eat 'em. They say they ain't no better brain food than oyster brain. Tha's why Al's so smart. An' so's Al." The 'Blob continued, "An' the shell holds the lemon squeezin's . . . we, that is Al an' me, we named those lil' fruits after our own family tree, Lemon bein' a fittin' name and such."

The 'Skull' bellowed again, "I'm Al."

"What do you do with the lemon squeezin's after you collect all of the juice?", Tumba asked. "Do you sell or trade it?"

"Tha's the best part", the 'Blob' squeaked, "We make the squeezin's, let 'er set for a spell, 'til it gets good and ripened. Al and me, we can tell when it's good and ripened, 'cuz it burns the smellin' unit when you sniffs at it. Then we takes a sip or two . . . or more. If'n we feels good and it puts us to sleep for a spell, we knows then that the squeezin's be just right. It kinda takes the hitch outta your get-along. Makes Al and me just smile to think about it! Then, we put that good stuff in coconut shells, set 'em by the trail a spell from here, an' there's those that comes and takes 'em."

"I'm Al", Al said.

"And what do they leave you in return?", Tumba asked.

"Did I say the other part was the best part?", 'Blob' hissed out. He took a moment to heave some of his bulk away from the fire after a couple of his green tufts had gone up in a flash. The smell was not covered by the lemon brewing. "Why, the best part is that since the dang fools don't know where we is, they can't see the camp. Don't ya see?"

Tumba didn't see.

"Well, since they don't know where we is, and they can't see the camp, then they jus' can't know we's outta lemons!"

"So, what is it that they leave you in return?" Tumba was getting just a little exasperated.

"I'm Al!"

"Why, missy, tha's the best part! They don't know . . . Wait a darn minute! you ain't the one tha's been leavin' us all o' them lemons, is you?"

"You mean, you leave the coconut shells full of your lemon squeezin's by the trail and they pay you with more lemons? That's how you're paid? For real?" Tumba was really wondering why she had never heard of these Lemons before. They were really too much!

"So, it weren't you, huh? Prove it!"

"I'm Al."

"Al, will you tell Al that I know who he is? Please?" Tumba was tired. She needed some food and rest. Maybe even some squeezin's.

"Al, she knows ya.", Al said to Al. Turning his talking unit back to Tumba, 'Blob' replied. "Missy, you still ain't proved you be the one or ain't be the one to be leavin' all the lemons for our squeezin's. Al an' me, we needs proof. This be our livelihood you be tamperin' with."

Tumba decided, that when in the land of Lemon, speak and do as the Lemons do. "Ok. Al, Sally, Mos'ly, Mr. Lemons, or however you're called, I have never had any of your squeezin's. And I have never swapped lemons for squeezin's at the trail a piece from here. And to prove it, the best part was if I had known, I never would have left you lemons since I knew how valuable they were to you, and if I knew, I wouldn't leave you lemons. And I know you need more lemons, therefore they're valuable to you. And I know because I know where you are. And the best part is they don't know where you are. So I can't be "they"! And I have no lemons! And I don't care where your great giant river oysters are or how you catch them! I don't care! I just want something to eat and to go to sleep. Please, Al."

"I'm Al."

"Yes, you are!", she tiredly recognized.

"We sneak up on 'em.", 'Blob' said.

Tumba sighed. "What? On who?"

"The oysters! They sleep at the river edge. They always be there, but we sneak up when they be sleepin'! Al an' me."

"And when they're awake, where are they and what do they do?"

"Oh, they be in the same spots. An' they be doing the same thing. They be thinking! Tha's how we knows they be so smart. But Al an' me, we just wait until they be asleep. That's the secret!

But, since your tribes, they be around us an' all, well, I don' guess Al an' me will have to kill ya. It'll be our'n. You an' me an' Al. The secret, that is."

With that revelation, and with the safety of her 'tribe', Tumba was the gracious guest and shared a meal of oyster brain followed by a healthy dose of the squeezin's. Yes, it did burn going down, but it sure did make a person forget her worries!

She slept like a baby, with not a trace of a dream. The Lemons had put her beyond her dreams . . . "I'm Al!" was the sound most delightfully deleted from her consciousness.

——————————

Morning arrived, and with it a wonderful change in the weather. The skies were crystal blue, a soft breeze brought the smell of the morning glories and honeysuckle vines from the river bank, and the spotted owls had vacated their posts to undoubtedly go to bother another traveler. Tumba retreated behind a tree to perform her morning ritual and instinctively looked to see if Org had left her a note. Of course, there was only undisturbed bark, but nonetheless, she felt a surge of hope. Last night had seemed like a bad dream with the Lemon brothers, and she felt things could only get better from this point on.

Walking down to the river to clean herself, she passed by Al and Al who had only moved enough to procure a few coconut casks of the squeezin's. Strewn about, a few of the shells had split open and Tumba noticed what appeared to be scorched areas all around them. The scene made her take a little notice of how her stomach could have survived such a rude guest, but surprisingly, she felt like a million flint stones wrapped in lizard skins. Al and Al would surely beg to differ, she assumed, if in fact they were still alive at all. By looking at them, that was questionable, but at their finest, it would still be guess, at best, if they were what one could consider being alive and well at any time in their existence.

Poor guys. Apparently from their clan lands the culture makes a practice of dyeing all of the freaks of nature this yellow stain and gives the family name of 'Lemon'. Must be a law, she figured. From that time on, they're considered outcasts. If only all Org-dudes were so easily distinguished, she pondered as she was splashing water all about her. They really didn't seem to be bad Lemons . . . in fact, the elders talk about beauty being only skin deep, yea, yea, yea . . . .

"I hope Org's skin isn't yellow", she said softly to herself. If it were, wouldn't she have heard about this dude since he had traveled so much in putting his tablets and signs about? The only rumors she had heard were all good ones. Thinking back on her feelings of the night before, she felt that she would, in fact, be in love with this Org if only they could ever meet.

But meet they would! Tumba had her compact disk, her determination, the sun, moon and stars to travel by, with the river leading the way.

Packing her meager supplies, she noticed a coconut by the spot she had slept the night before. Crudely scratched on the husk was the message: "4 MIS C—By!!—TAKE OWSTUR BRANE 2!!—LUV, AL/al". She then noticed a twisted palm leaf, appearing as an ear of corn, covered by green flies. Laying their love children, no doubt. Wrapped oyster brains! What a treat for breakfast! Tumba found a stick and quietly picked up her lovely farewell gift with it and tossed the palm leaf, babies and all, into the river from whence it came. Checking on Al, Tumba made sure they were all right, which they were in their own way, retrieved her coconut (the squeezin's really weren't bad at all!), and traveled on her merry way to get her Org.

With the weather cooperating, Tumba had made really good time by traveling along the river trail. With the sun at its highest, she decided on cooking a rabbit she had run down just a little earlier. As luck would have it, she came upon the remains of a campfire with dry tinder and wood laying right beside it. Putting her smelling unit to the ashes, she realized the camp had been vacated merely a few hours prior. "Definitely my lucky day", she muttered. It was then that she spotted something lying over the riverbank that looked vaguely familiar. It was one of those new fish catching contraptions! And the curved bone was snagged into a piece of driftwood. It was all in one piece, ready to be baited.

Setting her rabbit to be roasted over her fire, Tumba dug up some worms and figured on trying her luck with the contraption. "If I could get just a few fish, I could smoke them for my journey. I'm ready to get to Org!", she muttered to herself. Chewing on a rabbit leg, Tumba got her first strike on the fish catcher! It was really exciting! She let out and pulled in. She leaned to the left and then to the right. Rearing back, rabbit leg in her teeth, she whipped the rod up and over her shoulder, bringing with it one of the most striking fish she had ever seen. Scrambling up the bank, Tumba proceeded to remove the curved bone from the fish's mouth. The fish was almost the length of her arm and had a broad band of blue and pink running the course of its side.

It was a beaut! This one fish would be more than enough to send her well prepared and on her way!

Cleaning and slicing the fish into strips, Tumba placed the morsels on racks that she had made up using green saplings and vines after damping the fire to maximize the smoke. Placing the racks downwind of the smoke, she decided to relax and reserve a little energy for the trip ahead.

A little time had passed when she heard what she thought was one of those damned spotted owls hooting and screeching. Looking upriver from where the sound had come, she saw nothing other than a few starlings doing their acrobatic dances in their quest for food. Becoming entranced by their display, Tumba was startled by a soft voice behind her.

"I see you've made good use of my new state of the art fish catching contraption. Couldn't get the hang of it, myself."

Slicker than spit on a cave hide bone, Tumba wheeled around with her blade at the ready. "Get back!", she snarled.

"Whoa! Whoa! I mean you no harm. I'm sorry I surprised you, but I wanted to make sure you were friendly."

"Well, I'm not!" Tumba was getting into position to defend herself. "Go back the way you came and there will be no trouble. And get away from my fish!"

Backing away, with a smile on his face, Org replied, "All right, my lady. But I really had only returned for my fish catching device. Since you've obviously had better success with it than I did, keep it. And my blessings to go along with it." With that statement, Org turned on his heels and began to walk on, turning once to take in this beauty once more.

Tumba had noticed more than she had wanted about this intruder. He seemed to have a kindly way about him, and his equipment seemed to be in excellent condition! His lines were muscular and smooth at the same time. At least all of his sensing units were located in the right spots.

"Wait", she offered quietly.

Org slowed a little, but then continued on his way.

"Wait a minute!" This time she was a little more forceful with her request.

Org stopped and seemed to looking all about the area, everywhere but at her. "Did I hear a damned spotted owl?", he asked. "Those things seem to be everywhere today."

"No, it was just me. Wait a second. Were you baiting me with spotted owl calls? Making me look away when you slipped up behind me?" Tumba could maybe like this dude, after all. He didn't seem to care for those noise making owls, either.

Looking back over his shoulder, with a smile and a wink, he said, "Nah, that wouldn't be me. Must have been some other dude looking for his state of the art fish catching contraption. But since you've already scared him off with that blade and your surly ways, maybe you'd like to travel with me. Looks like we're heading in the same direction."

"Which way are you going?", Tumba asked.

"Home", he said. With that statement, he turned and headed off.

"Damn." Tumba wasn't quite sure what to do, but her gut told her it was all right. The elders' advice was ignored this time.

She forgot what the advice was, but it had something to do with strangers.

Gathering her smoked fish, supplies and her contraption, Tumba followed on, wondering what she was getting herself into and also trying to figure what they might talk about when she caught up to this dude.

———————

After a short time, Tumba caught up with Org but remained roughly a hundred bones behind. After all, this man was a stranger and it only seemed prudent to follow a little caution in such matters. Besides, she figured it would be a sight easier to check out his traveling abilities from behind: how he tracked . . . did he take notice of his surroundings . . . what stride was he most comfortable with . . . *my, he did have a nice rear end . . . did he just turn his head a little to check me out? . . . .*

But Tumba just shook off those silly thoughts. She had a destination to seek out and the goal at the end of the destination was this Org-dude so she would allow absolutely nothing to get in her way. She had really learned first hand at the previous show caves that she was right in the beginning! No distractions! No side shows! If this dude ahead of her helped her in her quest, then that was all the better, but there would be no hanky-panky or foolishness! She'd even give back that wonderful fish catching contraption rather than have any strings attached (no pun intended, she thought). Tumba decided to be cordial, at best, and neither ask for or give her name. *Yes, that was certainly the best way. No entanglements! No mixed emotions! Just traveling companions and that, like the elders liked to say, was that!*

Tumba, reaffirmed, strode to catch up with the dude. She was on to her 'Org'.

———————

She sure is a feisty one, thought Org. *Look at the way she's purposely hanging back . . . playing a little hard to get. I don't know . . . she sure has kept up with me . . . and after traveling a while herself, it seems. Good foot pad! I like that in a woman! And she sure knows how to take care of herself. The Gods know she sure is an easy one on the looking units . . . Really easy. But don't get carried away, Ol' Hoss, 'cuz she may be more than hard to get . . . she seems to be carrying herself with purpose . . . desire . . . like she's preordained or something. I'll just be cool. Yea, gotta be cool . . . I'll just sneak a glance to see if she's keeping up . . . slow down if I have to . . . Whoa, Nelly . . . this gal's all right! She's gaining ground . . . and fast. I'll pull over here to pull that thorn out of my foot pad . . . she'll see it and be impressed with my tread . . . I'll lean against that tree and cross my foot up over my knee so she can notice . . . .*

"So you're able to travel a little, then", Org muttered as he struggled with his teeth to pull loose the thorn. He turned his head a little more than necessary so this gal would obviously have to notice his macho endeavor.

"I'm not accustomed to carrying on conversations with men so obviously intent on having their foot in their mouth. Well, actually, that's not quite true, either, when I think about it." She couldn't resist a dig. "You must have soft pads to have a thorn go in so far. You really must not be accustomed to the trail", spoke Tumba. *Maybe I shouldn't have said that . . . but he's so obviously trying to impress me . . . macho pig . . . .*

Org stopped his pulling for a moment. That was mainly because of him gritting his teeth together and biting the thorn in two. *This woman is a piece of work . . . who does she think she is, anyway? . . . Like she's the expert on trails . . . what does she know about a foot pad, anyway? . . . Everybody knows that mine is the biggest and the best . . . she'll find out . . . cuckolder! . . . .*

"First trip", he said as he finished pulling the remainder of the thorn from his pad. "We'll be getting on, now". *I'll show her . . . .*

"Just a moment", Tumba spoke as she was setting her belongings down. "I really don't want to be off on the wrong foot. At least, I don't want you to. Just a little joke." *I've wounded his male pride . . . I guess I'll have to make amends . . .* "Do you think it possible that we could take a little breather? I have been traveling a little while and you do seem to be pushing it some." She watched his reaction: still a little firm. "Please?"

Women . . . they can be a burden sometimes . . . "OK-just a short one. Be ready shortly!" Org was feeling a little slighted, but man that he was, he did have a forgiving and tolerant soul. "What is it that you do when you're not traveling trails? I guess you're doing some needed errands for your clan." *Or her man . . . .*

Now, he's fishing . . . "I do have destination, although it has only to do with my business-nobody else's." *I'll give him a little, but not all . . .* "I received some information about a product that interests me, so I'm going to see about it. I'm just looking, though." *Maybe he's heard of this Org-dude . . . but he probably wouldn't tell . . . he has his own goods to sell . . . .*

"What product?" *I wonder what she's hiding? . . . .*

"It's something that I might want. Why do you ask?"

Because I could help you so much . . . just have to get some more facts . . . "Just friendly conversation. If you don't want to share it with me, that's really cool, but maybe I could help if you'd let me."

Yea . . . I'd just bet that he'd like to help me; like he cares . . . "Like I said, I'll just be looking. I don't know that I'll be doing anything for a while."

"Great! Maybe I'll just be showing! Are you looking for something cool or hot?"

"Cool."

"OK-do you want it to entertain you, or would you rather it was quiet and non-assuming?"

"Of course, I'd like to be entertained. Everybody likes entertainment!"

Org was on a roll. He thought he'd take a shot at another notion. "Would you prefer a four-legged or a two-legged variety?"

"Two-legged."

"Would you prefer that this cool, entertaining, two-legged variety to automatically do your bidding, or would you prefer to 'manually' get it going?"

"I guess I've always like to take charge at times. A person gets a little bored with things that are already there for her. I'd rather it to be a 'manual thing, as you put it." *Maybe this dude isn't so bad . . . he **does** seem to care . . . oh, well, I'll just follow this through and see where it leads me . . . .*

"Great! So you're looking for a cool, entertaining, manual, two-legged variety. Well, we'd better be going. I think I can help you. Just follow along, er, um . . . I'm sorry, I didn't properly introduce myself." *I'll just be a little professional with this one . . .* "I'm referred to by many as Mr. Gan, of the clan of Gan. We keep our caves at the far stretches of the great river where the land turns back to the high mountains." *That sounded strange: Mr. Gan . . . that's really my father's name . . . I'll ease up and make it more cordial, later . . .* "And you are . . . . ?"

"My name is . . .", Tumba hesitated, wondering if it was wise to let him know too much. He did seem genuinely concerned, however. Maybe it would be all right to give her name, but she wouldn't let him know how to get in touch with her later if he proved to be a con and a charlatan. ". . . Tumba."

"Well, Tumba, it's sure a pleasure! So, now that we're off on the right foot, let's get off on the 'right foot', as you phrased it, and follow me." With that, Org started down the trail with the correct assumption that Tumba would follow.

"So, Tumba, where do you hail from?"

A little white lie wouldn't hurt. "From way up north."

Org wondered why she would be traveling north on a quest if she was already from the north, but he decided, correctly, not to 'stand her up'. "I sure am surprised that I've never had your acquaintance, Tumba. I thought I knew of most everyone up there. I guess that's what life's all about, though: surprises! I sure am glad to have finally met you, though. By the way, how much are you prepared to give in acquiring this goal of yours?"

"If I can get the right terms, I have skins."

Org had heard of lizard skins being used as exclusive bartering tools in the southern clans. *So, she's from the south! . . .* "Assuming the terms are acceptable, how many skins are you budgeting?"

"If the product is the one that I've been seeking, maybe 250 skins. And no down!"

"No down?"

"Right! No lizard skin is worth as much as a downy lizard skin. From the flying lizards of the Tuuhie Mountains. I won't give up the downy skins."

"Fair enough! So if I can find you an entertaining, cool, 'manual', two-legged variety for 250 skins with no down, you'll be at your objective?" Org was getting more confident all the time. He was feeling that he could really help this Tumba.

Tumba was now walking side by side with 'Mr. Gan'. *He seems to know what he's talking about . . .* "Maybe. I guess I'll have to try one out before I make a decision. You seem to really know what I want. Do you?"

Org was thinking of all of the dudes that he knew of. Most of them would qualify for what she had suggested. With his help, of course. "I think so. I think I have in mind exactly what you need. Just be patient, and we'll see what we can do. Do you have anything other than your skins to trade? Perhaps an older 'variety'?"

"No other trade. That was another life. But remember, I'm just looking, and I really don't need anything yet, you see. I don't like to be pushed into a decision and I'll decide when I'm ready."

"That's cool!", Org replied. "I'll tell you what! If it's of no advantage to you, don't do a thing. If it doesn't benefit you and satisfy your needs-or your wants-don't give up your skins. If you can't see how others in your position have been rewarded, I won't ask you to do anything but be on your merry way. All I'll do is help you in any way that I can. Is that a deal?"

"Sure. That sounds fine with me. You know, don't take this the wrong way, but, well . . . you're a little different than most men I've dealt with in the past." Tumba thought about all of the show caves she had experienced on her trek. Then, she remembered the Lemon brothers. "Oh, Mr. Gan, I won't take yellow."

"Yellow?"

"Yes. Any other color but yellow. You know, like a lemon fruit?"

"Sure." Org had heard tales of this lemon, but he had thought it to be folk lore. "I wouldn't dare get you anything but what you really wanted. Guaranteed: no lemons or yellow."

With that, Tumba and Mr. Gan traveled forth to the north on their mutual quest: her satisfaction.

Several days had passed, and the two travelers had come to enjoy each other's company. A degree of respect had grown to one of mutual admiration, as well. True to his word, Org had indeed shown Tumba various 'varieties' on their way north. In fact, he had meandered a little to show her some other examples of lower bred clansmen. To his way of thinking, she had offered relatively little, so he would show her what her offer would get her in return. He introduced her to Ott, from the Cast clan, as his first offering of the journey. He did have two legs; in his own clan, he was considered cool; he wasn't yellow; he certainly didn't have an automatic desire to do anything; and the way that Ott could flick that bone from his smelling unit with his tongue and catch it with his eating unit *surely* was entertaining! After just a mere glance, Tumba had requested to move on.

"Mr. Gan, I certainly want more than that variety! He was so old!"

"Hey, Tumba. That's fine with me, since they're your skins. Let's move on and I'll find you what I think you want. I was just trying to get you within your 'skin' budget. Remember, you told me what you were ready to spend and Ott fit that amount, and I certainly didn't want you upset with me for exceeding your skins. Let's go!"

In spite of her spending the time to look at Ott, Tumba had felt her defenses tumbling all along with Mr. Gan. He was considerate, thoughtful, his hunting prowess was considerable, and his traveling ability was certainly the best she'd ever been around. He was, in fact, extremely entertaining, had two long legs, and was really cool, after all. He didn't assume everything: just enough, with a little of her prodding. He certainly didn't appear to be of the Lemon clan, either.

This Mr. Gan surely was worth looking into a little more. Who was this man, anyway? . . . Tumba was thinking less and less about her skins and was being convinced more and more of the value of this traveling dude she'd been fortuitously hooked up with. *I started out looking for an Org, and end up with a Gan . . . I wonder if he is available . . . it's odd I don't know, yet I seem to know so much and so little at once . . . but we're almost at the land where this Org is from . . . I'll find out from the local clans-people what Mr. Gan and Org are about . . . But maybe this Org isn't as important as I thought he once was . . . What does Mr. Gan know about this Org and should I ask him now? . . . .*

Mr. Gan, in fact, did know about Org and how Tumba came to be on her journey, since spying her hard disk with all of the information he had put out such a while back. He thought it amusing and odd that their paths had crossed the way that they had decided to keep his knowledge to himself, so as to better exploit his own worthiness and value. Tumba would soon share with him in his discovery but he first had to get her to appreciate him a tad more. *Sell her what I'm worth, not what the cost of getting me will be . . . .*

At the same time, Tumba was wondering just how much she'd be willing to give for the fellowship of Mr. Gan.

Since the time of the meeting between Tumba and Org, the weather had been perfect and certainly helped Org in giving him his bearings. Dependable bearings, you see, were also a prized commodity in any exchange during this time. Don't think Tumba didn't take notice of this fact, either. In fact, that was a major factor in her attraction to Mr. Gan, as she had marveled at how quickly they had traveled along with him leading the way. Perhaps it was also because of how much enjoyment she seemed to be having with his company, as well. Yes, the elders did say that events take the wings of the flying creatures when enjoying the events at hand.

And quickly it seemed, indeed, when Tumba and Org passed into his clan lands. Org took the time to point out local sites of

interest such as the 'Kick the Head Bowl', the 'bones exchange', a
local watering hole named "Squeezin's Squalor", the hide-trade
cave, and of course, the Cave of Wizer's Day. The Cave of Wizer's
Day was the place that Org had decided to finally rest and spend
a little time with Tumba talking of little nothing's: anything but
her transaction. Org felt it a good idea to have Tumba in a relaxed
state of mind before "getting down to business". He led her to a
raised boulder covered with soft hides and bade her to get
comfortable while he went to acquire some libations for the two of
them, leaving behind a tablet or two covering the exploits of the
Gan clan that conveniently had been on record and stored at the
Cave of Wizer's Day. There were more than a few entries that
featured the Gan clan's pride and joy: Org.

He hoped she would enjoy and relax. Oh, and to get to know
this Org, as well!

Only a little time had lapsed before Org (Mr. Gan) returned
and he was not unencumbered as his arms were balancing two
stone tablets, his hands held a coconut shell in each of them, filled
with "Squeezin's Squalor's" drink of the day. In his talking unit
was balanced a scribing instrument of a sort framed by a smile full
of teeth. "Ooo eee ooo aah aah, 'ing, 'ang, 'ahla, 'ahla 'ing 'ang", he
attempted to say.

"What was that?", inquired Tumba.

Org handed her a drink, set down his burden, and cleaned up
his talking unit appropriately. "I was just singing a little ditty.
Not much of a tune, though. Enjoy your drink. There was a special
on them today. It seems there's a special on what is called a "Lemon
Luau" today. Tasty. Drink up." Org took a swallow of his own
drink. "Are you feeling a little rested? You've had a hard journey."

Tumba set her drink down. "Well, yes . . . a little. Uumm,
good drink! I've recently had a similar drink not long before meeting
you."

"Is that right?"

"Uh-huh. Mr. Gan, I've been reading some on your family history, and I do have a few questions. For instance, there's a lot of mentioning of this fellow Org. Do you know this dude?"

"I might."

"Well? I mean, do you know him well?"

"As well as could be expected, I guess."

"So you know where this Org dude could be found?"

"I think I could accommodate your wishes. Are you interested in this Org, then?"

"Possibly." Tumba couldn't hide the smile that was creeping up on her face. "Is he as special as he's made out to be? I mean, a dude with his credentials would certainly be worth a lot-maybe more than some were willing to pay."

"Perhaps." Org was having a little bit of trouble in hiding his own smile. "And then again, at double what some weren't willing to pay, he would still be a bargain!"

"We're talking a dowry type of system, then? If the proper woman could establish enough of her worth, perhaps an arrangement would be established?"

"For the proper woman, for the proper amount, perhaps something could be worked out." Org was enjoying this as much as Tumba was.

"Mr. Gan, are we talking something within my means? I mean, I did tell you how much I was able to offer."

"Yes, you did. I'll tell you what: let me put some figures together for you on my tablets. I'll show you just how easily we can come to an agreement. This is the easiest part of the deal."

"Mr. Gan," Tumba couldn't hold it in any longer. "You *are* Org, aren't you? You are the Org Gan that is so touted in those tablets! You 'son of a gan'."

"The one and the only."

Tumba was amazed at the course of events that had brought her to be at this point in time. She really had been impressed with this Mr. Gan, troubled with deciding between Org and Mr. Gan. And here it was: one and the same! At this time, Org turned the tablets towards her. On tablet, one, a price was listed as to his worth. On a second, there were amounts listed as to how many skins with down would be needed. On a third, a smaller amount was listed. She noticed a fourth tablet that was lying on the floor untouched.

Org spoke. "Now Tumba, my going market value is 800 skins. Now here, you see on this tablet that with only 200 skins with down, as the skin lenders that the Wizers have appointed demand, your amount to be paid on every moon would only be twenty." With these words, Org shut his talking unit.

Tumba was amazed! *Who does he think he is? . . . I told him how much I wanted to spend . . . Maybe I should leave and go back to my own clan and forget this whole business . . . it's too much . . .* Tumba remained silent.

Org just smiled and said zilch.

Tumba glared.

Org smiled and said zilch.

These moments felt like eternity to both of them.

Tumba could stand it no longer. "It's too much!"

"What's too much?" answered Org.

"All of it is way too much!" Tumba was getting a little restless and was beginning to gather her belongings.

"Just relax a bit, Tumba." Org tried a different approach. "Look, I know you said you wanted to spend 250 skins. OK. Do you recall Ott?"

Tumba nodded her head.

"Well, he's OK, I guess. He would do your bidding, but he is a little bit older, wouldn't you agree? Is he capable of doing all that I can do? Maybe to a degree, but how long will he last? I don't know-nor do you! Look, how about if we forget the price: it's not important! Not at this point! Because if I'm not what you want or need, then the price doesn't matter. What if I could get you to give 400 skins with down and keep your moon payments at ten? You'd do that, wouldn't you?"

"100 skins with down is all I'll do. What's on that tablet on the floor? You didn't use it."

"Oh, that was for the trade-in. You didn't have a trade."

"You're really a piece of work, Org. OK, 100 skins with down, 16 skins a moon, you hunt, get me my Corinthian Mammal skins, wipe your pads before coming into the cave, and don't get caught up on every kick-the-head contest, and I'll think about it."

"Boy, you're a high pressure customer, Tumba. I understand how you feel. I've felt that way before myself, but . . . ."

Tumba cut him off. "Feel, felt, found! I've heard it before, Org. Besides, this wasn't the time and place to use it."

"What about the fish catching contraption?"

Tumba laughed. "Are you insisting that I keep it? I *am* the only one between the two of us that knows how to make something of it."

Org grinned: a toothy one. "I wasn't. But you're right. You would cook, right? Clean the cave? Rub my foot pads on occasion?"

"Rub feet? I don't think so, Org."

"OK. Listen, I do have to consult the elders about your offer. I know of your Total Reptiles Worked, but I would like to take them an earnest offer on your behalf to convince them to accept it. After all, I am in demand!"

"Yea, right! Here are two skins. That should convince them."

Org looked perplexed. "Tumba, if I were going to hunt one of your Corinthian Mammals, would you send me out to bring one down armed only with a twig off of a tree? Give me something to really show that your offer is a serious one. After all, I'm doing this for you."

"Yessir! All for me! Sure, Org, here are 18 more skins. Go and do your thing!" *All for me . . . right . . . Men! . . . .*

Org left the cave, only to return a moment later. "Tumba."

"Yes, Org?"

"Do us a favor?"

"What's that?"

"Cross your picking units for luck! We're going to need it!" With that remark, Org exited in a flourish.

Only a short time passed when Org returned accompanied by another fellow. Tumba noticed that his sitting unit was extremely wide. He immediately made use of his asset when he plopped to the floor.

"I certainly want to thank you for joining us in this proud land of ours, Tumba. In addition, I'd like to be the first to congratulate you on this great deal you've persuaded Org and me to do. I don't know how we even stay together as a clan doing these deals as reasonably as we do!"

Tumba was a little confused. "We have a deal, then?"

"Sure do! It's not **quite** as good as you wanted, but then, you did drive a hard bargain. You may have Org for only 100 skins with down and only 17 a moon! Plus the other considerations, of course."

That's only one more skin a moon . . . I could do that . . . I'll try one more dip . . . Can't hurt to ask . . . "I'll do 17 skins a moon. I'll honor the other considerations, as well. But I'll give you 50 skins with down, now, and 45 in one moon."

The man with the asset pondered her proposal a few moments, and then asked, "How many skins with down do you have right now? How much could you let us have at this moment? Not to empty your supplies, of course."

Tumba went to her leather bag and counted. "I have 78 skins with down on me."

"Tell you what I'll do. I really shouldn't, because my fellow elders may jump on me for this, but you give me 70 skins with down, and I'll do 20 skins a moon."

"I'll give you 70 skins with down right now?"

"That's all!"

"Make it 18 skins a moon and you've got a deal."

"I really would have to have at least 20!"

Tumba figured that she would push it a little farther. "OK! I'll think about it."

Asset man asked, "Think about what?"

Org stood silent, witnessing this bizarre exchange.

Tumba very sweetly spoke. "Mr. Elder", *my, he had such a large sitting unit . . .* "20 skins a moon is too much. Even 18 skins is pushing it!"

Asset man spoke. "Tumba, I have an idea! Have you ever heard of the family plan?"

"Not to my recollection, Mr. Elder."

"What if I could show you how to get the use of Org while he's a young, strapping man and not be burdened with him when he's old and costly to keep up? I could probably do that with only 45 skins with down and 12 skins a moon. You'd do that, wouldn't you?"

"No, I like to keep them until they're old and pull the remains from a ravine. I have done that before."

"What's that you said?"

"Never mind! Look, you have my offer! But I'll go a little farther and give 19 skins a moon and the elders throw in a celebration feast. Deal?"

The asset man looked hurt. "OK, I know I shouldn't do this, but you have a deal. Great! Now, Tumba, how were you going to handle your clan fees and your Title of Tribe cost?"

"I thought that was included. Title of Tribe? What's that?"

"Oh, everyone needs a title! We have to research what title would best fit you. It takes the elders, and of course myself, a lot of time and trouble to come up with the best title befitting you. It is for your own best interest, naturally!"

"All right, already! How much? Org, did you know of this?"

Org shrugged, gesturing towards the asset man.

"You know, these are busy times, but we could probably handle everything for only two skins a moon."

"And that's all there is? No more fees? No more charges? No Org rate, for instance?"

"That's it! For only 21 skins a moon, we'll handle everything!"

"Make it 20 a moon and that's it! Done!"

"It really pains me, but I'll do it. By Gan, have you got yourself a deal! Oh, and Tumba . . . . ?"

"What now?"

"Could I interest you in a program that would insure that your Org would be healthy and dependable?"

"Mr. Elder, no you couldn't, and thank you very much!"

The asset man thanked Tumba in return and left Org to finish the arrangements.

Org finally spoke. "Tumba, congratulations! You just made a great deal! I just have to record a few things on a tablet, and we'll be on our way to a glorious life ahead."

"Org, you had better be worth all of the trouble I've put into getting myself in this with you! Will this recording take very long?"

"Not long at all. And I sure plan on making everything worthwhile, not only now, but down the trail, as well. You just concentrate on the feast they're going to throw us. Oh, and Tumba?"

"Yes, Org?"

"Could I count on you for future referrals?"

And then the lights went out on our recollections of what Tumba's response was.

Epilogue

Tumba and Org lived their days out in almost complete harmony.

They took and gave between themselves continuously.

Tumba gave birth to six children: 3 little "orgs" and 3 little "orgettes".

And all of their "begats" begatted some more. Most are still begatting!

Through Tumba and Org's trials and tribulations, we've come to understand the value of negotiations and all of the good that becomes of it.

Through natural means and motivations, Tumba and Org achieved mutual goods and consequently a wonderful life. It set the stage for all of humanity in their future bargaining. It is indeed imbedded in the genes of mankind.

Certain steps were carried out in the conquest . . . certain steps that even today are being utilized throughout the world in buying and selling.

To achieve the wonderful and fulfilling ends that Tumba and Org staged for us, follow the evolved steps in acquiring the goals.

In order to have something taken, a form of presentation is required. Present yours with style!

It is your own.

But observe and take each step at a time.

Oh, and ain't our ancestors just marvelous?

CHAPTER 3

STEPPING INTO SALES

Hopefully, the tale of Org and Tumba was an amusing one. In addition, I hope a point was made . . . or rather, points. Notions that the business of buying and selling, trading and bartering, 'yinning and yanging', etc., are not held in the highest of esteem are certainly popular ones.

Thinking back to grade school, how many of us were asked just what we intended to be when we grew up? Who of you wanted to be a doctor? A fireman? A pro sports star? Astronaut, perhaps? Nurse? A lawyer? A car salesman?

A **car** salesman? Yea! Right! Unless your family was already an owner of a dealership, who in their right mind wanted to be something like that? I'd rather gut fish; direct traffic in Singapore; sing a duet with Roseanne at a nationally televised game!!!!!!!

In fact, there are few things I can think of that I'd rather not do. I mean, really, who in the world wants to volunteer to be thought of as a cheat? A vulture? A con man? Slick Willy from Chicago?

Well, there are a few of you who really get off on that, I guess. Indeed, I have met a few of you. But, take notice: you are in a great minority!

I have met so many wonderful people who are making an absolutely wonderful living dealing in an incredibly wonderful career. Many of these folks had no idea that they would ever be in the position to appreciate what a marvelous career choice they, in fact, had made.

College degrees dictated that they follow a choice made at the age of 16. Maybe it was the age of 20. Whatever. In so many cases, the lucrative future didn't seem so promising, after all. Falling back, unwilling to wait tables any longer, or perhaps stock shelves, an ad was answered which beckoned to the car business.

The car business? The place everyone hates to go. Do people hate to go there because it's felt that there is no other choice? Maybe only the shadow knows.

Anyhow, I digress. Many who choose to get into the car industry may do so reluctantly, feeling as if it may be the last straw. Some are beckoned because of the carrot dangling, offering huge incomes. Others do it to kill time until something better comes along.

Some stay.

But most leave.

Why? Is it the negative responses they receive upon meeting customers walking up? Are the hours longer than expected? Do they resent the grind they happen to be under? Are they disillusioned with customers after believing a few "untruths"?

I guess these are a few of the reasons many choose not to remain in the business. I'm sure there are many more. I also know that I have thought about where I would have been had I started with the car business as a career had I started at an earlier age.

I would have been wealthier. My satisfaction would be increased. My 401k would be busting at the seams. My real estate holdings would be free and clear.

So, it will just have to wait until tomorrow. I still remember coming in as an outsider. I still am an outsider. But my allegiance is now divided between the buyer and the seller. Actually, that is really okay with me, since I so have an advantage in realizing the mutual points of view. I can and do wear the shoes and hats of the buyer, but detachment to make a reasonable profit is easily obtained. What is a reasonable profit? It depends on the value of the product to the buyer. I'm a true believer in selling the value after which the profit is fitting to the deal.

So, let's go to the beginning but after Org and Tumba. Let's look at our own beginnings and see how we have all been conditioned to what we may have thought to be a unique situation in the buying and selling of cars. Maybe you could call it good old-fashioned horse trading.

As a student, whether we realized it then or not, we shared a mutual goal with the teacher. We learned our subjects, the teacher in turn was rewarded with satisfaction and was paid to do so. The music teacher instilled the sharing and the love of music to be rewarded, again, with the satisfaction and pay. Maybe a transferring of thoughts and skills is in itself a feeling of immortality. But giving and taking are what's important to this example.

We are all conditioned to learning in school at an even younger age by developing in steps. The obvious are: crawling, walking, toilet-training . . . they are all mutual goals accomplished between child and parent. A skill is performed that perhaps was learned as a game.

The athlete carries this on even as the coach relishes the team's and individual's victories.

All that we experience are in themselves fundamental, mutual directions. They all begin with, and are in and of themselves, the infamous first step of a thousand mile journey. A goal had been focused upon and measured steps had been taken to reach mini-goals through progression.

Remember, a dog has never been properly trained by kicking it when the trick wasn't performed. Usually, rewards of a kind word or a biscuit have the positive result desired. I'm a biscuit guy, myself.

Sometimes, no matter what the good intentions may be, there are objections that do arrive. A child may fall down and begin crying at the failure, hurt and pain of not being able to walk yet. With a little love, cajoling, or perhaps the lure of a toy, or biscuit, the child may try again; and yet again, until the first step is accomplished. Mutual give and take.

We all achieve through want and need. Sometimes it's the ones influencing us who have the most want and need, but goals are always in pursuit. In grade school, perhaps the teacher's ultimate goal is to have the student achieve an appreciation of the literary greats and expansion of their own worlds through the love and joy of reading. It all starts there with first, the learning of the alphabet; the distinction of consonants and vowels; how they co-exist to form a meaning: learning how to spell 'cat' and then 'cats'. Through continued progression, give and take, time and effort, and perhaps no little amount of fun, the word 'catharsis' is derived and understood. Its root remains, however, from the letters of the alphabet and the word 'cat'. Cataclysm, catacomb, catastrophe, catamount, catalytic, catbird . . . on and on, ad nauseum. We learn, we expand, we build upon, but the truth remains: without the 'basics', the end product suffers. I mean, after all, just what is an '-aclysm'? Or an '-acomb'? Maybe a way to part the hair of one who stutters?

Learning to play the trumpet begins with the rudiments of the music scale and learning where low 'C' is and how to apply that note to the trumpet with the right lip "scrunch" and valve depression. (This is not a psychological state in valve therapy). Actually, the valves remain open (like you care, but the record needed to be set straight). The notes are learned, up and down, all around, the flats, the sharps, they're mixed, timed, "staccatoed" and "crescendoed". They are put together as three notes to make "The Indian Corn Dance" song. Very basic, indeed. If you've ever been to New Orleans and listened to good jazz and blues, these same three notes are used continually in the most intricate of melodies that soothe the soul. The basics are still ever-present to be expanded upon but can never be ignored or forgotten. Really! I'd bet that those of you who have been to Bourbon Street and were so "hair-lipped" that you may still be in a Zombie-like state would even agree. At least stare back and blink 'yes'.

The better the foundation, the more sturdy the house. Keep the 'Cat' in your steps and don't forget your basic "scrunches".

Odds are we'll all grow older (but as Jimmy Buffett suggests, not necessarily 'up'). So, just in case we do, it may not be a bad idea to "calendarize" your priorities and the "steppes" of your 'negotiated' accomplishments.

Guide yourself and dream to where your focal point co-exists with your goal. We all come to forks in the road of life at times. Which way did they go? Which way did they go? (Say preceding two lines with a "dufus" accent). How does one know which direction to take if there is no idea of where one wants to end up? It really is a pretty simple concept when you stop to think upon it. The high road may take you to the mountains whereas the low one may take you to the shore. Do you want to end up as high on life? Or perhaps cool and wet is your dream. Just know what it really is that you want and take the steps to get there. Want to play trumpet on Bourbon Street? Learn the music scale and simple songs and step your way upwards. Want to read Melville? Or Shakespeare? Or maybe Stephen King? You get the picture. Maybe if you do read Stephen King you'd rather forget the picture.

Steps . . . steppes . . . the time it takes to get there . . . an achievable goal at a time.

Run a 40 yard dash in 4.3 seconds? Have a .390 batting average? Pitch a no hitter? Have triple doubles? . . . Dives rated at 3.3 degree of difficulty? (Think . . . or thwim!)

These are, yet again, paramount in achievement and athletic peaks by learning in steps. Steps that were negotiated; filled with humbling trials and errors . . . Yet, these achievements were filled with fond memories. Looking back, maybe one could refer to them as the three 'F's: Fun, Frolics and Fantasy.

Let us not forget the three 'D's: Dickering, Devotion and Demands.

Nor the 'E's: Ends (by means), Evolution and Excitement! ("Deese" 'E's).

Remember, we all have unique experiences, likes and dislikes, abilities and frustrations. There are individual talents that took years to develop in all of us. Seize that core of which drives you and let your years of investment in yourself return dividends a thousand-fold. We have all negotiated continually to get to the point of who we all happen to be. There have been infinite progressions of development through learning, training, rewards and in some cases, negative reinforcements.

We have all tripped while learning to walk and run, but skinned knees and all, we still hold on to the premise that getting there is half the fun. Sometimes, it may be ALL the fun. That being the case, chuckle, collect, co-exist, cogitate, countermand, and catch the next coach to the carrier of cranial (if not carnal) capabilities. Remember: "Can't" DID die in the cornfield!

Post script: the previous collective cant is an example of a lot of collective 'C's. You will learn about three others further on. 'C's, that is.

For those of you wondering, yes, I *am* high on the car business. The real car business. The real "Any" business, perhaps, but we'll play specific 'cars and trucks' shortly. Be patient.

I just want to lay down a foundation for success in the car field and also point out that the automotive field really is not any different than others in relating to the human endeavors involved. It takes learning, experience, good instruction, a good attitude (check-up from the neck up), patience, and perhaps a little talent. But with a goal in mind, all of these are self-inspired. As to the goal . . . what roads and steps are to be taken? Is fulfillment of life your goal?

One inspiration that has worked well for many is to envision the "figurative" day after fulfillment. Imagine your short-term goals as a present complete with wrapping and bows. Rip off the bows. Shred the wrapping. (I loathe people who save their wrapping!) Toss it out! Feels good, don't it? Then, relish the accomplishment. Is your goal having your credit cards paid off? Buying a new car for yourself? A house, maybe? Laying hundred dollar bills down for a new guitar? Buying your mother a car?

Whatever your own gifts to yourself may be, these are all miniature goals. They are set, thought upon, scheduled, and accomplished. Any thing is possible by setting these individual steps.

And guess what? They add up. One step after the other. Steps to the stars! (Not a misprint: I didn't mean 'stairs').

And you are always getting better. You are improving upon that of which you've built. An old Chinese proverb states something like this: "Man who adds and improves upon house lives forever; when finished, he dies." In my words, "keep gettin' on gettin' on". It is fun, healthy and gives a reason to wake up in the morn. You just may have to "worry (that you'll) . . . be happy".

Yep, sometimes it really is a "Catch 22". Just suppose that you are too successful; too independent; too fulfilled . . . .

My gosh, your friends may envy you . . . or admire you . . . maybe even like and respect you! The worth you feel of yourself may be overwhelming! It really is tough to be happy, but somebody's got to do it!

Make your life a novel with you as the main character. Develop a few secrets from yourself to create a few cliffhangers. Keep it interesting and fun. But keep those goals just a hair out of reach. Some refer to it as a 'carrot'. That's cool. But I like cliffhangers. More poetic!

NEGOTIATE. Breaking down that word, one divides the four syllables into their proper pecking order. To whit: NE: Latin for not having. Maybe it's Greek. Or Lithuanian. Whatever! But it damned sure is ne-gative!

Moving on:—GOT: to have, as in "What you 'got' on your head, you bald headed sucker . . . a toupee or a bird's nest?"

Now to:—IATE: the combination or acts of the preceding sum of forms. As in, "I can't believe I Ate the whole thing!"

NE-GOT-IATE!

Negotiate from within yourself. Negotiate your terms. Negotiate your tools. For everything, there is a season, so dress and act accordingly. Season your being!

Achieve the belief of yourself.

Achieve the empathy and perspective of that or whom you wish to persuade.

And it all starts with listening—both to listening to yourself and to others. Remember, communication is unspoken as well as spoken, so fine tune your senses! One then continues with ongoing attempts and the grasping of the perspective that one is confronted with to understand the path and direction to a mutually satisfying goal.

All of this can literally be obtained through love of not only the mutual benefits before you but through sincere love of the principals themselves.

I know, Mother Theresa and Will Rogers were two of the few who loved EVERYONE, and they were exceptional, but bear with this concept. Granted, there are those we know that are commonly referred to as a person that only a mother could love. That is fine and good. But remember, you are not placed in front of a person to judge his or her values and the placing of said soul in the "Good and Wholesome People Hall of Fame". You are, however, in said presence to bargain and to negotiate on a deal of some sort. Don't, DO NOT, get involved in a "pissing match". Yea, I know! It is tough. You don't want your friends and peers to approach you later and say, "I wouldn'a let him say that to ME!". And, "Man, I would've told her I got her @#$%^! RIGHT 'CHERE!".

Yep! They would've won, all right. The battle! What about the "war"? The deal? Your mutual objectives? Were they satisfied?

Probably not.

So the immediate goal would be to gain common ground, wouldn't you agree? So, in starting for that common ground, wouldn't it make just a little bit of sense to start out with someone you really cared about?

So, do that. Care! Be patient! Keep the immediate goal in mind!

You know, I dare you to think of someone in your past that maybe society judged to be a less than perfect citizen. You know,

that person that everyone said, ". . . he was always nice to me.
Who woulda guessed?". Or, ". . . but she was such a good mother
to her children. A regular church-goer, too!". In spite of your
personal feelings and the fact that you thought he or she to be
really okay, jail time was maybe all that person had to look forward
to for a while. But still, ". . . he woulda given ya the shirt offa his
back. Musta been a mistake!"

You knew the good parts of these folks and you naturally looked
for them. If you knew a bully in high school that bullied everyone
but you, and in fact, treated you to an ice cream cone after school
daily, you would judge this dude to be a stand up kinda guy! A
real stud! Maybe you didn't agree with his other actions, but you
probably felt everyone else misunderstood him. Except for you!
"Cuz he didn't whip your butt." He was really okay!

Point: if you perceive a person to BE good, you will look for
the good in them. When you find that good spot, concentrate on
it. If the only good spot happens to be an admirable belt buckle,
concentrate on that point when you feel your feelings beginning
to go awry and you really want to give him "what for". It really
works! Try it at home, boys and girls.

You see, it's really hard to hide your true emotions. People really
do pick up on false flattery. So, don't flatter! Give sincere, heartfelt
compliments. If you can only come up with one, so be it. At least it's
for real. Now, the person truly feels the sincere need and want that is
felt by you for his best interests. Fact, boys and girls.

So now, you've made a friend. Now, in the words of Monty Hall:
"Let's make a deal (. . . I chose my apparel, I wore a big barrel, and
they rolled me to the very first row . . . I held a big sign, 'said 'Kiss
me, I'm a baker, and Monte, I sure need the dough' . . . ."

So, I grabbed that sucker . . . by the throat . . . until he called
on me . . . "Cuz my whole world lies waiting, behind . . . door
number three . . . .). Thanks to Jimmy Buffett!

Just what does the customer perceive to be behind door number
three, anyway?

Well, let's see. By now, you should have stopped the customer,
looked at a common objective, and listened, listened, and listened!

Listen to what is communicated verbally and non-verbally.

Listen to what is said and not said. Watch for body language. Check eye movement. What communication existed when the car drove onto the lot? Or when it was left parked down the street? How were you greeted? Or were you ignored as the customer tried to out-sprint you in the opposite direction?

It is ALL communication. How it is perceived is another matter altogether. In the words of past warriors, "Know thine enemy!" Do not make the mistake of thinking that I am referring to the customer as the enemy; rather, the lack of communication is. Perhaps, the misreading of the message is the enemy. You have to think on your feet, so you decide. Further on, I'll give some of my interpretations of the "lingoes" of the customer, later to be referred to as an O.T.D.B. (Opportunity To Do Business) or otherwise known as an "Up". The customers, that is. Not the "lingoes".

So . . . You're Thinking of Selling Cars
(Or anything, for that matter) for a Living . . . .

First and foremost, remember the fact that most of "us" hate car salesmen (sales people: P.C.). They're a step below a cock-a-roach (although it is held in some quarters the evolutionary cycle places a car salesman well above an attorney).

"They're vultures! They lie! They cheat! They mislead, misdirect and missed the bus on the morals collection trip!" (Editor's note: printing was already ongoing when we realized our error in including the previous excerpt out of text. Rather, it is a phrase taken from Roc's forthcoming guide to government that is entitled: "Pholiticians: Their Phits, Phollies, Philandering and Phibs!")

Secondly, some surmise logically that these sales people attempt to victimize their customers. Logically: a key word! Now, wait just a minute! Is there a reason they are in fact selling cars? At birth, a slap on the behind and magically the tongue happened to turn silver? Mystically, six fingers developed on both hands? A wink then turned to a nod?

Point in fact: as previously suggested, the overwhelming majority of us, by human nature, I might add, are indeed sales people, salesmen, sales ladies . . . persons of sale. I repeat: by nature, we are all into selling by some degree! We *were* all are born to sell and to be sold as well. It's in our genes! From the earliest of times, as in Org's and Tumba's lifetime, existence depended on the bartering of tools, trades, and trinkets. Often, the most elusive of idea, schemes, trade routes, and even people themselves (as in the world's oldest known profession) were exchanged for maximum profit or advantage. In recorded passages of the 'Lewis and Clark Expedition', Meriwether Lewis gives evidence to the importance of buying and selling by the very "grocery list" he created in preparing for this historic journey. In addition to the basics, such as armaments, shelter and transportation articles, Lewis included trade tools, in the way of colored beads, ornamental clothing, medallions, craft tools, and various other items that were deemed equally important in securing their safe passage through the Louisiana Territory in their quest for the Northwest Passage. In order to reach their goal of crossing transcontinentally, accords had to be reached each and every time contact was made with the Native Americans en route. Trade goods were used to establish communication, friendships, new trading partners for future mutual benefits, and hopefully, an allegiance to the new "Father" in Washington, D.C. Of course, as far as Lewis and Clark knew, lacking the goods to trade, they could have well been "Lewis and Clark-a-Bob". (As in 'Shiskabob: dead-style!) They had to sell themselves and who they were representing. They were indeed the sellers.

But, in being the sellers, they were the buyers as well. Remember: give and take!

There is an entry in their journal that refers to when they were nearing their goal, horses were required and when negotiating for some much needed "horsepower", Lewis stuck a magnificent bargain in acquiring three excellent horses for what amounted to $20 U.S. at the time in trade goods. Both sides saw the value in the exchange. Lewis was happy, the Shoshones were happy.

After going on their way, Clark found he needed more horses. The Shoshones, knowing they had a captive market, negotiated a little differently. The price of horse trading had just gone up! They were willing to sell, but they decided the value of the horses was a little bit higher! So did Clark. For one horse, Clark had to lighten his load by one hundred rounds of ammunition, a knife, and a pistol. One can only imagine the value placed on such items in the unexplored wilderness!

Eventually, twenty-nine horses were negotiated in a deal. However, Lewis and Clark were "out-yankeed" in trading as they ended up with nearly all of the twenty-nine horses having sore backs, "pore", or "young". Seller's market.

And you wondered about the origins of the used car dealer? The concept is as American as "Mom and apple pie". Who knew?

In a nutshell, where there is a market, a product will be created. It takes people to supply both the market and the product.

There is, has been, and always will be a need for transportation. Hence, the market. Furthermore, what are their other needs? Now, and in the future?

The product has been produced.

For now, leading into the 21st century, the most popular means of transportation is the automobile.

There are an awful lot of people out here, guys and gals, who need to get somewhere else in a certain manner and style.

Someone has to help these people. Automobiles are sitting around. Some folks are still walking.

Help to get them together.

Be magnanimous!

Be a Car Guy (new P.C.).

Perhaps?

So . . . Just Where Does One Start? . . . .
(And is it justifiable as a career yet?)

Well, who do you know in the car business? Anyone? How about the dude or dudette from whom you most recently purchased your last vehicle? Or a friend of your landlord? Have you checked out the classified? Who do you consider to be the "best" dealer in the area?

Okay! You've found an 'in' to a dealership! Now, what is their training program all about? Are the sales people "thrown" on the floor or is there a bonafide process by which employees are trained to learn and grow?

Yes, there are stores that use up and throw away the "meat" (a.k.a. new sales staff). After the sales person has "met and gret" the "Up", taken 'em for a test drive, and then returned to the dealership, (for those of you still wondering, "met and gret" is the past tense of "meet and greet"), the customer is introduced to a 'closer' to finalize the deal. The salesperson returns to repeat the above while the "system" takes care of the previous customer. Ad nauseum! No training . . . no skills enhancement . . . but "be nice" and smile! And get 'em in. *Really* cool!

In addition, one may get the 'pot lot'. Typically, this is a used car store that with the help of the experienced sales staff, one may learn in short order "everything" there is to know about the car business! Get 'em in and out in a "new" car. Nothing to it! Piece of cake! No follow up! No concern of customer satisfaction (at least, not after the car has rolled)! Roll 'em up and move 'em out!

Well, at least these people learned something . . . albeit a dubious "something".

There is also the new breed of 'Superstore'. These stores have grown popular of late due to their 'hassle-free' approach of "one price" shopping. For the most part, this type of store has been more of a used car store, but many dealerships have applied the one price approach to new cars as well. There are attributes to this approach, but in my humble opinion, I think the biggest impact will be with better service for the customer. Competition prevails! Great! However, folks, guess what? Some studies have shown that where these stores have 'popped up', used car prices in the market area have increased by about $500! Good for the dealers! Great for you, too, if you happen to have stock in them! Really nice people make their living in sales at stores like these. Ask them if their commission is based on that extra $500 . . . *No?* . . . didn't think so. The store did okay? Great! Take Aunt Jenny's inheritance money and invest. You may get your just rewards that way, but sales staffs in these pay programs typically get 'flat' sales vouchers. That is regardless of the profit. That may sound great to some customers who aren't willing to ask for more for their trade and less for the "new" vehicle, but the sales person is merely an order taker. That's okay. Some people don't survive "confrontation". More jobs are open for a greater segment of the population because McDonald's and Sears have full sales staffs. So if this is what you want, go for it! Feel great that you are a part of the greater 'whole' that is affecting the car business as it's been known! Evolutionary!

One question . . . just how high do you wish to fly?

Are you one who likes to be part of the crowd, or do you have enough faith and self-assurance to go into business for "yourself"?

Do you want to help a person with their transportation needs, or say, "That's the price . . . sorry you can't afford it. Good-bye!"?

Do you want to be part of a system that would appear to monopolize the market and give no room for negotiation? To assist and be under-rewarded?

If so, your learning session is over. Quit reading! Close the book! Go home! Do Not Pass Go! You could, however, collect $100 or maybe even the famous $200 by going to work at the "Superstore". Nice talkin' to ya!

We weeded a few out, eh gang? That's cool! They were, and are, nice people. I'm sure! So if you're opting to stay, let's assume that one of these days, you may be helping them into a nice vehicle after they get "crapped out" in their new profession. After all, some need extra help on three or five hundred a week.

So let's look at a store that I consider an ideal place to work. How about one that sells new and used? A store that services what it sells? One that has a well stocked parts and accessories department? A dealership that has a rental car department or conditionally supplies loaner cars? Nice looking inventory and grounds? Professional appearances by the staff?

Training for new employees? That is, training that's available to new employees that is furnished by the dealership and not paid for by the employee. One that the dealership, not you, pays for. One that has a continual training process in place with coordination with the manufacturer it represents.

In other words, a dealership is desired that puts value on keeping a person that is well trained and gainfully employed as opposed to one that prefers to keep untrained personnel. If you were the owner, would you rather keep untrained people? Hiring and firing? Remember, these people (you, perhaps) are representing the organization. Each employee is the infamous "weakest link". An establishment that understands that is one that is going to have an ongoing process to ensure that their personnel are second to none.

That is the type of dealership attitude that you should search for and be associated with!

Wow! You stopped reading and went out and found one! Good for you! Now, I assume you are starting your training soon. Perhaps I can now help supplement it.

Congratulations, by the way!

CHAPTER 4

SOME BASIC INSIGHTS

There are, indeed, basics that are needed in the car sales profession just as it is in any other occupation. The first objection a salesperson is going to have to any sale, however, happens to come from an unexpected source: from his or her own mind! Some refer to this as ATTITUDE! Logically, what is needed is your absolute conviction that what you are doing with your life is not only all right, but it is part of an ideal that is absolutely necessary in carrying out what has been a tradition throughout history. It is what makes the human species tick! It rounds out what our society happens to be! We have been, we are, and we will be a society of barterers, traders, givers, takers and candlestick makers.

Survival itself has perpetuated itself upon the give and take of things we possess for the items we have craved or needed. Who among us have not needed a screw to repair the dresser? A book to know how? (Hopefully, this edition would be considered one!) The screwdriver and drill to perform the work?

Who hasn't paid the banker for use of money?

Who hasn't bought a ticket to a football game . . . a movie . . . or a concert?

If one follows the progression of give and take (negotiating), an absolute myriad of transactions, trades, barters . . . to get to any given event or material of substance, one finds it is all give and take. *ALL* of it is!

Yet, returning to the automobile salesperson, perhaps there are traits in many of them that made them successful to begin with. There are many merits existing in other professionals that seem to be apparent in the most successful of car dudes and dudettes.

For example, a common trait of merit of a G.P. (doctor, folks) is a calming bedside manner. The same is true with the successful car salesperson. The ability of a trial attorney to present a case and point of view, to counter objections and to present positions to a judge and/or jury is certainly an attribute for continued success. Ditto for the car salesperson. A psychiatric counselor has to present his/her case to the client in such a manner as to be beneficial to the overall well-being for subsequent success. Again, the car salesperson.

Go to the house of God and the confessional houses a negotiation of everlasting peace between priest and parishioner. Agents negotiate rights and rewards for their clients, whether they are sports figures, actors, political aspirants, or merely the unemployed (the unemployment office would be their agent, guys).

The cars sales position is one that requires the donning of many hats! Get the picture? The same skills that others require to be successful in their respective positions are combined in the person that is striving and succeeding in reaching success.

Commit! Believe! To yourself! In yourself!

How do businesses justify profits?

Let's see . . . we all read. Right? Let's take a look at paperback books. Typically, they are sold for maybe an average of $7.95 each ($10.95 Canada). Now, what do you suppose the cost is for paper? Forget the marketing, shipping, taxes, author's contract, etc. A want or need is fulfilled. People purchase for those fulfillments to happen. A story is told and life may be just a little bit better.

We pay maybe 89 cents for a metal bolt at the hardware store. It might weigh 1/4 ounce, yet we seldom consider what steel costs a pound. We need the bolt, we buy it and we apply it. Seldom does one ask the clerk the store's cost of the bolt before justifying the purchase. It's relatively small, so we buy: no questions asked. The bolt isn't bought for the simple act of transacting a purchase— it's bought for the services the bolt will accomplish!

The same can be said for pharmaceuticals, pool supplies (golly, now they can be high!), tire outlets, dog snacks, travel arrangements, etc.

The point is, we ALL buy and sell daily, weekly . . . for all of our lives!

So then, what makes the buying and selling of cars stand out so significantly? What separates the purchase of a car from the other actions we take in everyday life and makes some of us swear, sweat, shake, vomit, and have a propensity for loose bowels? Sometimes it's merely just the thought of the crossing into the 'Badlands' at XYZ Motors!

Perhaps it's in the customer's believing he's making what many consider the biggest buying decision outside of a home purchase.

Perhaps it's in not wanting to commit to a binding agreement and feeling an obligation that subsequently limits any financial freedoms: feeling life's future being squeezed . . . all future life in dire jeopardy.

Oh, bleak feelings!

Maybe there is a question as to the proper choice of vehicle. After all, there are over 400 new models available to choose from in the U.S.

Maybe, if the person does know which car he wanted, the dilemma persists: did I pay too much? Is it less elsewhere? Did I get screwed on the trade?

Is this the best dealership? I mean, really, no wonder the people today can be so neurotic!

The right salesperson? AAAAHHHHHHHH!

The right salesperson! Now *that's* an idea!

What makes the right salesperson?

For starters, maybe it's a matter of addressing the customers' fears (yes, fears!)!

Simply put, we all have a fear of doing the wrong thing: fear of resulting instability . . . fear of wrongful selection. Fear of rejection: "Will they even *give* me the loan?" Fear of ridicule: "You paid *what?*" . . . 'I wish I had known . . . *I* would have paid more for your trade!" . . . "You *obviously* haven't heard about all of the recalls your new car has had!" . . . etc., etc.

You know, I guess even more simply put, we could say that we all have a fear of the "Boogeyman"! And guess what! The "Boogeyman" stands right behind the car dude! Sometimes, it's just like the "Invasion of the Body Snatchers"! The customer thinks the salesperson may well be possessed! AAAAAAArrrrrrggggggggg gggghhhhhhhhhhhh!!!!!!!!!!!!!!!!!!!!

You *do* remember the "Boogeyman", right? Throughout man's history or woman's *her*story (1/2 PC), the "Boogeyman" has resided in hollow logs and dark burrows reeking of stench and decay . . . he's been troglodytic by nature . . . .

The "Boogeyman" has ridden the crest of the storm. He's harnessed himself to the swirling maelstroms, only waiting to dismount at the doorsteps of emotions . . . .

He's resided amongst the Ancient Mariner's debris, ruminating to surface and become airborne as the wings of an albatross . . . .

He's been locked away in the tombs of pharaohs, breathing his sour breath upon the souls of the unwary . . . .

It's even recorded in the annals of time that he's been hiding, and waiting, as intrusive a creature that's ever been, in your very closet . . . .

. . . . at night . . . .

. . . . when you thought all was safe, cuddled in your warm, protective comforter . . . .

(Baby Boomers: did "The Thing's" hand ever wait for you under *your* bed? . . . *Still* scares me!)

(Generation X'ers: we're talking Peter Arness here . . . the original . . . in black and white . . . sorry, folks, I digress . . . .)

Anyway, the "Boogeyman" exists, feeds, and perpetuates himself on the unknown and ignorance of: 'What If?' . . . 'Could It?' . . . 'Should I?' . . . .

The "Boogeyman" stands right behind, and maybe inside of whom? You got it!

The Car Salesperson!!!!!!!!!!!!!!!

So, exorcist type dude/dudette . . . do your thing! Eliminate the "Boogeyman"!

How, you ask? Well, you want to sell cars for a living, right? Okay, then, just . . . *Turn On the Light!*

They have questions: you have the answers! They don't know: you do, or you will find out! They can't or won't? Ask why or why not! Help them! Help them! Help yourself and your team!

You see, it's just a matter of education. We all make the best decisions on the best input. We all feel secure in knowing the obtainable options and resulting consequences of our decisions. Given most or all of the "known", the unknown (the "Boogeyman") is vanquished! The educating of the customer has systematically dismembered the "Boogeyman" limb by limb, casting doubt to the four corners of the earth.

However, before the earth feasts on dismembered body parts (new "hook" for a Stephen King book: dibs on rights!), it would be well advised to speak the "Boogey" language.

You know, I do realize you have yet to learn the basics of car sales if you're just getting involved, but these are thoughts for you to ponder while you *are* learning. Think on how the directions of the steps of selling can be applied as you learn them. For those of you reading this to check on yet another 'jag-off' writing a 'how-to' book, pick the "Boogey" of your choice and persevere. The preceding was an editor's note, don't ya know!

Now, onward and upward to Boogey 101! To talk the language of Boogey, one has to first understand Boogey. Actually, most of us really do understand the language since we are ALL customers at different places and times. What is needed in the position of being in the work force is to *recognize* Boogey when it is spoken. Where one is to infer the implications! Yepper, when you catch the ball, make sure the pitch back is comfortable to the customer: he's already felt the size of the 'ball'; he's thumbed and fingered the seams on it . . . he's even put a little *Boogey* on the curve he's attempted to throw. It's up to you to make the return comfortable for him to continue to handle. Remember, YOU are the professional and have been accustomed to your 'home' work place. Use the comfort you feel in your own surroundings and transfer same to your customer. Toss the ball back gently at first. It's warm up time: protect your pitching arm. Here are a few examples of *Boogeyism* and how it's spoken:

Boogeyism

1> "I'm just looking."

2> "Not buying today: just started!"

3> "Just my lunch break and I'm killing time."

4> "My car's in service and I'm killing time."

5> "I'm waiting for the year-end clearance."

6> "We have to get our children at the day care center, but we'll be back."

7> "My husband/wife has to okay the deal . . . but we'll be back."

8> ". . . . have to pick up the mother-in-law at the airport, but I'll be back."

9> "I'll buy when my (color, transmission, option, style, gender, religion, lucky V.I.N., pick 'em) is in stock!"

10> "When the rate is right!"

11> "LOOK! I don't want any games!"

12> "I really don't want to waste your time."

13> "I'm just looking for a friend of mine."

14> "I'll buy when my (tax return, inheritance, bonus, lottery, horse, ship, Barbie doll investment appreciation, Gila monster, pick 'em) comes in!"

15> "I was just driving by . . . thought I'd look around . . . be back after I get something to eat."

16> "I just want the bottom line!"

17> "Just give me a ball park figure."

18> "I'm just shopping, now!"

19> "I'm shopping for my company: a committee will have to approve your best price!"

20> "*Nobody* pays sticker!"

21> "Let me sleep on it."

22> "Too High!"

23> "I'm not going to lease!"

24> "I don't have my trade with me."

25> "Well, what I want to do is pay off my trade ($3,500 inequity with customer thinking $2,000 equity) and use it as down payment, no cash, and reduce my payments to $235 dollars a month."

26> "I've got your deal beat!"

27> "I can't afford this!"

28> "Is this your best deal?"

29> "You're not giving me enough for my trade!"

30> "I'll give you $100 over invoice!"

31> "I want to sell my trade first."

32> "The 'Book' says (according to the oh-so-reputable Banker) my car's worth more!"

33> "You'll give me the same deal next week!"

34> "I'm waiting for the rebates to get higher!"

35> "I *HATE* car salesmen!"

36> "It's too hot!"

37> "It's too cold!"

38> "Not today, but when I *do* buy, you'll be the one I do buy from, 'cuz Ah like you!"

39> "I read in a car magazine that Motown-Jipuzinny Motors is coming out with a new model within the next decade, so I want to wait for that!"

40> "I *know* I can't get this model without the do-wicky option but I don't need that. I'm not paying for it!"

41> "I want the same color car as Michael Jordan drives!"

These are but a few (really, customers can get extremely creative! Can't you, when you want to?) of the examples of *Boogeyism* that you will hear both on the lot and in the booth. Your mission, should you decide to accept it, is to translate their *Boogeyism* into reasons to buy. Give Hope for Gain! Cause and effect! For every reaction, there is an equal and opposite reaction. Everyone, even the biggest of the infamous 'lay-down' (The dictionary defines 'lay-down' as one who accepts your first and most profitable offer, or 'pencil'.) is going to have at least two or three objections! Let them win, but overcome their *Boogeyism* with that of your own.

Here are a few suggestions to offer to your customers when they speak "Boogey", but remember, there are an infinite amount of ways to speak the language and this is, after all, "Boogey 101". Use your imagination, but appeal to the customer's own persona.

For example, possible responses to the preceding list of 'Boogeyism':

1/   **"I'm just looking"**
    1a/   "Great! I'm just showing!"
2/   **"Not buying today: just looking"**
    2a/   "Great! And what are you looking for?"
3/   **"Just my lunch break and I'm killing time!"**
    3a/   "Wonderful! If you don't totally succeed in killing all of it, would there be some remaining when I could be of assistance?"
4/   **"My car's in service and I'm killing time!"**
    4a/   "Well, thanks for giving us a chance to fully assist you! Would you be interested in alternate payments? That is, paying on a vehicle under warranty rather than payments with service bills attached?"
5/   **"I'm waiting for the year-end clearance."**
    5a/   "I certainly can understand that! However, some folks don't realize that dealerships control their own fiscal years, and thus their clearances they may offer to the public. Allow me to show you what's available even now! You *did* mean you wanted to save, didn't you?"
6/   **"We have to pick up our children at the day care center but we'll be back."**
    6a/   "Alright! Let's take the vehicle you were interested in to get them! Let's see how it works for your entire family!"
7/   **"My husband/wife had to okay the deal . . . but we'll be back!"**
    7a/   (Similar to 6a above)

8/ "... have to pick up my mother-in-law at the airport but I'll be back!"

    8a/ (Well, I'm not sure about this one. Mothers-in-law scare me. Give hope for gain!)

9/ "I'll buy when my (color, transmission, etc.) is in stock."

    9a/ "What if I can give you what you *really* want: that is, most of what you need at a true value?"

10/ "When the rate is right."

    10a/ "Great! Because we can get the best rate available to you *right now!*"

11/ "Look! I don't want any games!"

    11a/ "I agree! Let's find the vehicle that is right for you! I assure you, price is the easiest part of the deal."

12/ "I really don't want to waste your time."

    12a/ "Wonderful. Nor do I want to waste yours! Just what goals are you out to accomplish?"

13/ "I'm just looking for a friend of mine."

    13a/ "Is your friend named 'Peter Pick-Em-Up'?"(Just kidding: maybe the car or truck MAY be the friend, but play by ear.)

14/ "I'll buy when my (tax return, bonus, etc.) comes in."

    14a/ "What if I could save you money by buying now and defer payments? Then, you could use that money for a trip or home fix-ups?

15/ "I was just driving by ... be back after I get something to eat."

    15a/ "Fair enough. Wait! I apologize! Were you expecting our free dinner at Luigi's with a test drive? Come on!"

16/ "I just want the bottom line."

    16a/ "I certainly can understand that! But if I don't show you the concern to make sure your wants and needs are met by thoroughly showing you proper vehicle, a bottom line isn't reached. You don't make decisions based on price, alone, do you?"

17/ "Just give me a ball park figure."

    17a/ "Well, Sun Devil Stadium holds about 65,000 people! (Whatever ... similar to #16a)

18/ "I'm just shopping now."

    18a/ "Great! And just what is it that you're in the market for?" Two door? Four door? Five speed or auto? AC? Stereo? Marvelous!

19/ "I'm shopping for my company: a committee will have to approve your best price."

    19a/ "Fair enough! We deal with most of the major corporations in the area. They are well aware of our great service, parts and body shop as well as our great deals on the purchase. Does your business consider time to be money? Let me show you the advantages others have grown to appreciate!"

20/ "*Nobody* pays sticker!"

    20a/ ". . . and you would not be expected to! Aside from the price, is this the vehicle that would fit your wants and needs?"

21/ "Let me sleep on it."

    21a/ "I can understand that. But wouldn't it make sense to have assistance in making your decision while you're here with professional guidance? After all, what can the pillow tell you that you haven't already learned? Is it me? (No) Is it the vehicle? (No) Is it the monthly/down-payment.? (Probably—the 'Boogey' objection is now isolated, so overcome it!)

22/ "Too high!"

    22a/ "Compared to what?"

23/ "I'm not going to lease!"

    23a/ "Fine! If you want to pay more, that is a choice I can respect." (Leasing conversions discussed later on . . . .)

24/ "I don't have my trade with me."

    24a/ "If we could work out the details to your satisfaction, based on your description of your present vehicle, would you be interested in a great value? Now?"(or) "No problem! Let's go get it!"

25/ "Well, what I want to do is to pay off my trade (it's 'upside down') and use it as a down payment, no cash, and reduce my payment to $235 a month."

25a/ —(Show customer just what vehicle would work on that particular budget. This is 'Step Selling and will be discussed later.)

26/ **"I've got your deal beat!"**

26a/ "So it appears! But, are we comparing apples to apples? Are we comparing the same trim level? Is the vehicle new or used? Is it a demo? And, although I wouldn't expect you to be informed of this, but at that price suspicion of repaired body damage should come to mind. Not necessarily true, but possible! Wouldn't you agree?"

27/ **"I can't afford this deal."**

27a/ (Assuming customer is 'carred up' properly) "I can see where you would feel that. Other satisfied customers felt that way at first. But, if you can't afford this payment/down payment, can you budget a new transmission/engine/etc. repair bill all at once? Let me work to tailor this deal a little better to meet your satisfaction. Okay?"

28/ **"Is this your best deal?"**

28a/ "No, *my* best deal would be if you gave me $9,845 over M.S.R.P. Nobody has given that much to me yet." (But it would probably be better to shift focus to value: "You are not going to make your decision based on price alone, are you?")

29/ **"You're not giving me enough for my trade!"**

29a/ "I understand where you might feel that way. If it would benefit you better, sell the trade on your own. We would be accepting your trade for your convenience." (You could ask how much they received when they last traded in their toaster, TV, stereo system, shovel, family pet, pet rock, or shower head. Make your point, and then show advantages to expedite car deal by *including* the trade. Perhaps sales tax savings could be applied to further customer savings. You may even ask if they have anything else of value to reduce the amount of financing, such as their pet rock.)

30/ **"I'll give you $100 over invoice."**

30a/ This is up to the discretion of the dealership. If it is a unit that must be moved, i.e. an old-age unit, a purple/

pink/green car, etc., well, $100 over would be delightful. Considering incentives, rebates, hold back, etc., this could be a lucrative deal. On the other hand, sell the value of the vehicle again. It's 90% selling, 10% closing! Remember that!

31/ **"I want to sell my trade first."**

31a/ As in 29, work the trade in and out of the deal. It depends on whether or not you're pitching or catching! Go to the Gap close (to be discussed later) and make the deal, with or without the trade. Other closes will be discussed that will affect this deal as well.

32/ **"The 'Book' says (according to banker) my car is worth more!"**

32a/ Explain how wholesale and retail works. Consider reconditioning, local market value mileage, fuel economy (Gas Mileage close),Switch from price difference to payment. Or vice versa. Read the up and coming closes and apply as needed. (Ask the question that since the banker has all the money: let the bank buy it . . . they set the price! Right?) But *DO* show interest in the buyer's needs at all times. Ask how the pet rock is doing!

33/ **"Oh, you'll give me the same deal next week."**

33a/ Set a limitation on the time period. Are incentives expiring? Are there rebates? Is the 'book' about to change on the trade value (down, of course)? Are the dealership's advertising supported discounts about to go? Is it a slow day? Do you need this deal for you to win in a sales contest? (Contest close: later.) Is the car last of its kind? CREATE URGENCY!!!

34/ **"I'm waiting for the rebates to get higher."**

34a/ Same as above: CREATE URGENCY!!!

35/ **"I *HATE* car salesmen!"**

35a/ "I can understand that! This is why we have a different approach at our dealership! At least, *I* have that ideal. If you can't see the benefit of doing business with *Roc Motors*, or why we sold x number of vehicles last year, or showing you our award winning service department, etc., as many of your friends, neighbors, co-workers, relatives have, I don't expect you to buy a thing! In fact, I wouldn't permit it! (You may even want to remove you badge at this statement, demonstrating that you are one with the customer. You are making a deal that the customer should like: you're a "customer" that is working 'under cover' just to help plain ol' folks like him/her!)

36/ **"It's too hot."**

36a/ Compared to what? (Hot deals, business slow, show off AC, offer beach vacation, etc.) CREATE URGENCY!!!

37/ **"It's too cold!"**

37a/ Is now the time to show off your great AC? I don't *think* so, Tim! (You decide!) Probably best to show why otherwise adverse weather conditions make for *remarkable deals* for the consumer!

38/ **"Not today, but when I *do* buy, you'll be the one I buy from 'cuz I like you!"**

38a/ . . . Sorry, dudes and dudettes! But buyers are liars, it's said. Maybe justified, maybe not, but you have to pull out all stops to make the deal NOW! It is wonderful to make friends, but there are a lot of really nice people who don't make it in car sales because they won't ask for the SALE! Study the closes! Remember, they are there to BUY! Give them a reason to. Switch "shoes" (another close) and work as hard as possible to benefit their needs. You certainly would appreciate that if your sales representative did that for you! Wouldn't you?

39/ **"I read in a car magazine that Motown-Jipuzinny Motors is coming out with a new model within the next decade, so I'll wait for that!"**

39a/ Yea, right! Surely, into all of our lives, a little rain must fall, but this is just good old fashioned selling. Look in the dictionary—under salesman. It says something like: "One who persuades." Create urgency . . . (a little understated this time . . . getting tired). Oh, and cars are NOT unlike computers in that they are always bettering safety, emissions, performance, etc. When that new model from M-J Motors *does* arrive, just what would this dude be waiting for then? Sell what is real and now, guys and gals! It don't get any better than this!

40/ **"I *know* I can't get this model without the do-wicky option but I don't need that! I'm not paying for it!"**

40a/ "What you are saying, Mr. Customer, is that if you don't have to pay for the do-wickey, you would like to buy and drive this car home *now?* Let me see what we can do for you." (If the customer doesn't want the do-wickey at all, and if it just cannot be removed, you're on the wrong car. Switch the car. If that doesn't work, go into partnership with the customer in designing the 'perfect' vehicle. Or sell what is real. Whichever would be easier. You decide!)

41/ **"I want the same color car that Michael Jordan drives!"**

41a/ Easy! M.J. has a car of every color! But all of the cars are black at night! Who cares? If they insist on Robin Williams' color, just give Robin a call and have him talk to the customer to justify the color you have in stock. His number is 1-813-555-MORK. Yes, I know there are always new and unused objections that arise daily. That is the way of any of our languages. They evolve! Why should "Boogey" be any different? It isn't. So adapt, learn the language, and read on. This book is devoted to that very subject.

Let's Boogey!!!

Now, don't forget what *Boogey* is. It is really an obvious conclusion that by countering the *stated* (or *real*) objections, your alternatives should always take the approach of keeping the customer's interests and benefits in mind. A normal, negotiated exchange relies upon the emphasis of *gain* to the customer, not the forfeiture or sacrifice therein.

No healthy relationship can thrive, whether it be personal or business, without give and take; benefits and exchanges! Take notice that the concept of compromise is merely for the reason that compromise exists by two or more parties mutually *losing* something. (An exception to this statement could be made at a voting board meeting of S.I.A.M. (Self-Inflicting Association of Masochists.)

For those among us who are not exactly thrilled by the idea of body clamps and such, a normal, friendly (albeit sometimes *excited*) exchange of mutual ends is certainly recommended. I give: you take! You give: I take! No give/give! No take/take! The short term is not the suggested goal! Remember: should anyone in a negotiated process be cheated or scorned, they probably *will* find out about it, only to never want to do business with you again.

It is a matter of addressing the stated objections and bringing the *true* objections to surface. By negotiating, one can bring the objections to surface and light. To and by all of us! In car vernacular, (that professionals do not use with the public), even "Larry and Lucy Laydown", along with their neighbors, "Gary and Gretta Grape", will *always* have some objection. Address it . . . give back what is needed . . . *satisfy all parties!* Done! Simple! Well . . . not always . . . but the principle of give and take has held true since our beginnings and will continue to do so.

So, be true to principles. Live by ethics. It is said that the true measure of one's honor is what he would have done if he were never observed nor caught at it. (P.C.: you, too, ladies!)

Somebody *is* watching! It is also rumored that someone also said that it is perfectly fine to make a fair profit.

To make a prophecy, proportional profits are predicated on preparation and just how prevalent your procedural presentation is proffered! (The Wizers said that, I think.)

The key? I guess the above shows an obvious use of 'PR'! (I know: corny, but true.)

The profits come to both sides and in direct proportion to how those you have dealt with have profited by the making of your acquaintance. Hopefully, there are high grosses on both sides of the fence. That's only fair! Wouldn't you agree?

CHAPTER 5

*Prospecting . . . (or getting your face in front of
their faces so you will be in position to help their lives
be a little better for having met you!)*

You know, a person could be the best in the world at closing a deal, but starve to death if there were no deals to close. It really does take two to Tango! Also, three are required for a *menage a trois* and four to make a foursome at the golf course. You get the picture (no dirty minds, please!).

Actually, as silly as it may seem, the aforementioned could be cases of prospecting. In selling anything, be it cars, mortgages, shutters or shingles, people can always be in the market for what you may have to offer. First, they *do* have to know just what it is that you *do* offer.

Many businesses, of course, advertise by way of radio, newspaper, television, flyers, internet, etc., and by way of these customers frequenting your place of business, anyone can trip over a deal.

But what sets the truly successful salesperson apart from the rest? Numbers!

That's right! Pure and simple. Numbers!

One has to remember: the dealership or business that you are associated with has been successful due to the fact that it has been doing something right just to be there and to remain in business. Typically, the car dealer has a projected monthly and annual goal of sales and will hire enough people to meet that goal. Most dealers will set a realistic goal of eight or so sales per salesperson per month to meet what is realistic for that dealership's particular market and will hire accordingly. That's two a week. At an average of three hours per deal. Six hours a week.

Six hours a week? That's all? I mean, that is *easy*! Another piece of cake!

It surely is. Easy! A person can make $1,000 to $2,500 a month that way.

Easily!

However, I don't think you would be wasting your time with my bantering about if you were the type of person that would settle for average and except what the business is merely handing you. I think you want to be better. Be different. Stand apart. Stand proudly. I think you want to be standing as a representative of your own enterprise. You are the only one, remember, that can produce as the result of your own experiences. You just know how proud you would make Org and Tumba, don't you?

You really want to stand on your own two feet (my dad used to tell me that standing on your own two feet was usually much safer that standing on someone else's feet!)

What is your name, anyway? Insert here: ( )'s Auto Sales! This is your business, after all. We all have rules and regulations to follow, regardless of our respective station in life, so take the responsibility of being successful and self-reliant! Depend on Number One! That would be you!

Take advantage of the fact that your dealership supplies inventory, bookkeeping, placing the vehicles in their proper site, maintenance, service, and management!

You just have to get the numbers! You just have to get in front of people!

You just know that you want to help them, don't you?

Just think how fortunate anyone would be to deal with someone as worthy as you are! You *are* the *best*! They broke the mold when you were made!

You owe it to the world to help out whenever you can. You are a regular Albert Schweitzer!

You just have to let these people know where you are so they can be relieved of their burdens. You have to follow Org's example and prospect. In the modern sense.

I would venture to say that there are more suggestions by many of you as to how to find people, but some of the tried and true ones that work well are here for you to use. Don't be limited! Anything that you may imagine can be the ticket to just one sale and that is one that you would not have had otherwise.

At the dealership, you do have an obligation to take your share of customers when your time comes up. Most dealerships have an orderly method of making sure that all salespeople get their share, so hence the tag of "Up" on the customer coming in. (As in baseball: when it's your turn to bat, you're 'up'.) Just do not refer to a customer as an 'up' to his or her face. Also, do not use the verb tense of 'up', as in: "Oh, hi. Glad to meetcha! I'm glad you could come back with your wife today. I was sure impressed with her when I 'upped' her yesterday!"

One may get undesired consequences when the word is used in that manner! Be assured, as well, that it is in no way referring to "one upsmanship"!

Moving right along, here are a few suggestions for making contact with folks:

1. Make an acquaintance with Alexander Graham Bell! Sometimes, he may not be held in high regard by those of us who hate to work on the phone, but it is an efficient means of communicating on a personal basis. There are those so good that they can make cold calls from the phone directory and

have decent success in setting appointments. In areas lacking efficient mass transit this is particularly true since there is a higher average of licensed automobile drivers. This is an exercise that is better started with someone who has some experience in calling since an example can be followed.

I know from experience just how heavy that phone can be when it is first picked up, but keep at it! The phone does get lighter, I promise!

a) There are better sources of phone numbers, folks. The above example is calling at its hardest. Just wanted to get it out of the way. From the dealership, ask for a list of past customers. Remembering that most folks trade, turn in or sell their cars every three years or so gives you a chance at calling satisfied customers who like the product your dealership offers already, presumably likes the dealership well enough to have bought or leased before and can perhaps appreciate a follow up call from that very place of business. At the very least they can be reminded just how quickly time does fly! They can be made aware of any special offers (aren't they all?) your dealership has on a limited time basis. You are looking for the "hook" to get them in: don't sell the car, sell the appointment!!!

Common sense will dictate in which direction you will go with your enticements: safety, performance, fuel efficiency, computer do-dads that weren't even thought of just a few years ago. Faster, higher, stronger, lighter . . . superlatives to pique the buyers' curiosity enough to have them want YOU to show it to them.

b) Call service customers. Your buddy, the service writer (remember him or her? You bought that lunch for him? Stopped by when things had slowed a bit to share a joke? Promised a "bird dog", AKA referral fee for any customer?) has that car that will be MUCH more costly to repair than at first anticipated. Why not avoid the middle man, take the trade in service 'as is" and drive the new "Za-ZOOM' model home today? It beats waiting a week or more and than just driving an old 'has been', doesn't it? A deal or two a month can always be depended on by following your service buddy's lead.

c) Call the dealership's 'Sales Log Book'. The more organized dealerships will keep a record of all of the potential customers who passed through the dealership. Perhaps a test drive was taken, perhaps not. Maybe the customer was "just looking" and wasn't lucky enough to meet a salesperson. Maybe, maybe . . . Follow up with a call and an enticement. Just don't tread on a fellow salesperson's toes while doing it. Maybe they are following up, as well.

One way to find out if a customer is being followed up on is to call the customer and ask. It is appreciated. Except by the lazier salesperson who DIDN'T follow up. Be prepared to confront an attitude adjustment with this person if you received a paycheck he should have had. C'est la guerre! There are "orphan" car owners out there. Adopt them!

d) Have any friends? Family? Past co-workers? Know your pharmacy dude? 7-11 dudette? Neighbors? Family doctor? Grocery store clerk? Pool guy?

Call any people you may know that already know YOU. They can't give you business if they don't know just what it is that you are doing for a living, can they? Call them! Give them your card and ask if their mom, dad, brother, vicar or health training specialist need wheels! Promise that "Bird Dog". This dog DO hunt, brothers and sisters!

e) Ever looked in the classified ads? Where people sell their own cars? For money? I wonder if they might be thinking of replacing it? Avoiding the hassle of getting "screwed" on the trade? Ever think they might be tired of the nightly calls from people who can read just well enough to know the car is for sale? Who may ask the seller if they could pay in installments?

Maybe this person selling a car could be enticed to having your "used car buyer" taking a look at it and offering cash for it. Maybe that same amount could be used for a down payment. Maybe a step could be skipped and just have the car traded in for a possible sales tax advantage. Maybe . . . .

f) From your past experiences and occupations, you have perhaps had customers or clients who were very satisfied with your performance before. Look them up and let them know where you are and what you are doing now. Why wouldn't they love to deal with you again? You're the best, right?

g) Businesses and business owners are good places to prospect. It just depends on your nature as to whether or not you may want to enter the psychology of the "Fleet" salesperson. It is absolutely fine to approach these sources on your own. Keep in mind that you may want to gather any and all personal information on your clients, as always, should you enjoy this so much that you move on to the Fleet Department down the road. These customers, when treated fairly and efficiently, want to come back to where they made it happen before. You are particularly expected to be a complete professional. Typically, one may expect more than one vehicle sold with a business relationship. Check the Yellow Pages . . . .

h) Are you a member of the Elks Club? Rotary? Kiwanis? Church? Synagogue? Bowling league?

These, and other organizations are great places to be known in as "the Man" when you want to be automatically approached. Talk about good referrals! People feel much more comfortable when dealing with "one of their own". Don't you? When Joe gets a good deal on a car, Suzie wants to know where he got it. He tells her. More importantly for you, he tells Suzie to just deal with YOU! Because you made it happen! Referral bases are the best system of doing business. Period! When a business (yours, remember?) produces a good product for a fair return, most people are proud to let others know about it. People, by nature, like to be associated with a winner and this is an example of how one may relate. It's your business, and by extension, you are a winner. The deals are smoother, more smiles prevail and profits are usually more just based on the fact that you've previously done a good deal for someone already known. You are not only trusted but relied on! When they day is done, you feel good about yourself and how you have helped a really good customer.

You get paid well, too.

Call whomever you know. Do it daily. Make it part of an organized schedule. One hour. Two hours. Whatever. But fit it into slice of pie that is part of your day and do it with consistency. Whatever you accomplish, it will be far more than if you had never had the acquaintance of Mr. Bell and his invention.

2. I have mentioned 'bird dogs'. That is a term merely used to shorten the word 'referral reimbursement'. Easier to say. That is a financial 'Thank You' to anyone who refers a car buying customer to you. It could be $50. It could be $100. It could be whatever amount you and your dealership felt was a reasonably good "enticer" to encourage folks to refer buyers to you and yours. I have had a few bird dogs come my way in my time and it surely is nice to have those pennies from Heaven. I just sent a friend or acquaintance to someone I knew. Heck, if they were going to buy a car anyway, why not from my buddy the car salesman?

Offer them freely to people that can send a little business your way. You may be lucky to find a "professional bird dogger" who makes a point of selling his associates on you just to make a little spare change. A little that turns into a lot! For both you and for him!

The dealership smiles a little, too . . . .

3. Mailers (as in 'snail mail').

As in any creative advertising, there are a myriad of ways to present oneself. I think one of the rules of thumb that needs to be adhered to is to be "differently entertaining." There are companies that can be contracted (which your dealership most certainly has, and is, working with) which will mail hundreds or thousands of flyers, postcards or letters on a termed basis for a contractual cost. The return of contact of something of this nature varies with the "approach" of the mailer and certainly that depends on how much is to be spent. Most starting in the business wouldn't want to be strapped with a huge initial outlay of funds.

This type of advertising may get, on the average, somewhere around 2%-4% return with a reasonable approach so obviously great numbers are needed to get good results.

To cut costs, a buddy system could be used with someone you work well with and could be even more effective.

As in other advertising regarding your place of work, remember to get an 'okay' through the management before mailing anything. There are laws in place in your area that you may not be aware of. You may be certain your very competent management team is on the ball and knows everything there is to know about how to say a lot without wasting space and time!

For you creative types, a periodical is a really nice touch. I have seen great results with the use of this type of mailer. Essentially, a mini newspaper is created to perhaps catch your customer's eye before it is deposited in the trash bin. That is another secret to any success: staying in front and in "the eyes of the beholder".

If one were to send merely coupons or flyers, only the people interested in the product might even take a glance. This is not to say they don't have results, because they do, but I am talking of something a little bit different here: something that will delay the trip from the mailbox to the trashcan.

This is on a little more personal basis, I guess, since it is geared to past or current customers. You are not a totally anonymous entity at this point. This is geared to put your name in front of a face and keep it there just a mite longer.

However your creative little mind may work, use it. But here are some thoughts you may want to use. Keep in focus to your objective, but remember there is no direct sale here.

a) Have an article on new product features from the vehicle manufacturer. It could be the new vehicles themselves, new safety features, bells and whistles heretofore unavailable, new accessories, etc. Articles can be obtained through he dealership that should be of the eye catching variety.

b) Perhaps some personal notes would work for you. Write about items that may seem to make you a "real" person. One that we'd all be glad to know and meet! A photo (some of us may have a face made for radio . . . be careful!) may be a nice touch. Don't overdo it, though.

c) Word games, crosswords, anagrams . . . etc. may be what some people would hold on to for a while. Make your own if you want.

d) A section for recipes could perhaps be something the great chef would like to clip and keep around. It could be a regional thing (Mexican in the Southwest, Thai if you happen to live in the Far East). Be advised, this could lead you into a new career if you happen to be more talented in culinary arts than you had realized!

e) A joke or two or three could be a nice touch. Be cautious with your choice of humor, though. What may strike you and your buddies as hilarious may be insulting to some of your customers.

f) "CAR"toons could be an eye catcher. If you're so inclined and artistic you could try your own hand at it.

g) A coupon or two would work. Perhaps a coupon for a "bird dog" or a night at a nearby resort for your next (paying) customer referred to you would be a nice addition. Again, use your imagination!

h) Maybe some service specials. Work with management to get a coupon for oil change specials, lube jobs, etc. Have an addendum to entice the customer to reach you for an appointment. Your service tech will appreciate your efforts, as well, and be more likely to refer more of his or her customers to you.

Remember that these are just some suggestions and they are, in fact, tried and proven to work. If you merely get one extra sale a month out of your efforts then you should surely consider it worth the while. Put your thinking cap on and come up with something on your own that will not only help with your success but can be fun in the creation. Today's user-friendly computers and their programs will help even those of you who are a little challenged with your creativity.

4) Internet. I guess that is a little obvious but I happen to think the internet is a tool that is better used once you are established. There are so many options for advertising on the net and they are changing all of the time. Web sites with pertinent information are certainly examples of a method used frequently.

The problem I see with a Web site is that unless one is devoted to making it stand out, it can get lost in the "forest". To be unique takes a fair amount of time and updating continually. That is not to say that it can't help: it can. I just want you to realize that is why your dealership (the bigger ones, at least) has a resident "geek" or two on payroll just to continually monitor, update, correct and tweak their own sites to keep them as effective as possible.

Look into it if that is your cup of tea. Again, just look at the cost versus the returns. Once you're established and making a steady income, the thought of paying an outside source to do just that may cross your mind.

5) Referral bases. Perhaps you are at dealership that has records that are in an organized fashion relating to the sales and who sold what. Actually, if records could be pulled that show a particular salesperson's customer base, that source could be immediately applied for your own use as the salesperson's "replacement". I am referring to a salesperson who is no longer

employed at the dealership and has stranded yet another group of "orphan owners". You now have an instant base of folks to get in touch with, stop by their place of work (since you were in the area) to meet them and give them that bottle of touch up paint that you bought from the parts shop at a discounted price. Oh, and by the way, are there any of their coworkers that may be interested in what the auto market has to offer today? Maybe the offer of the free trip to your local (or exotic) resort for a test drive? Set the appointment! Make a good first impression!

I guess I would have to say that there are really no limits to the ways that one could prospect. All of what I have suggested DO work! But, boys and girls, there are more. You just have to figure them out and let me know!

In all seriousness, follow the examples of those around you who are successful. This can't be said enough! There is a reason that these people make a lot of money. Remember also not to be embarrassed . . . more likely than not these folks are glad to show off their skills. It is nice to be recognized.

But do learn how to prospect. There is an old saying, "Anyone can cook a trout. The trick is in catching it!"

Not enough emphasis can be put on making appointments for your customers. There is so much more ease on all sides when dealing with someone that has already made an acquaintance. Whether it is by phone, mail, referral or internet the customer already has somewhat of an idea as to what you are about. You, as well, know a little about your customer. Proof, again, is in the pudding.

Anyone may check their stats at the dealership. It is virtually certain to show that appointments will buy from 65% to 75% of the time! Great, ain't it?

Walk-ins (Ups) buy 6% to 8% of the time.

Which do you want?

Do remember, if you do your job properly and take your share of Ups, make the sale. Don't believe the numbers I just showed you.

But . . . in the unlikely event that you don't make the deal the first time (I know you will, anyway!), you now have every reason to follow up and make sure you tie down an appointment to make the deal later.

Make sure you sink the hook when you do. Give the customer every reason to want to come back and deal with you!

Make the sale!

Continuing on, let's just see what we can do about our fine folks when we do, in fact, have an opportunity to do business!

CHAPTER 6

WORKING A SYSTEMATIC APPROACH

FOR CONSTANT SUCCESS

Otherwise Known as Steps to Success

It has been said that practice makes perfect. That being said, no person, or system, can be perfect. We are unique and we face unique circumstances constantly. But, there is no denying that anything worth doing is worth doing well.

Few of us have a crystal ball. At least, one that can foretell the future; and that, my fine feathered friends, is what one would need to be able to fine tune all of the varied situations that could be up and coming in your endeavors.

In lieu of a crystal ball, we have a brain that allows us to think on our feet. We have original approaches to any given situation and the ability to adjust with the flow.

Given all of that, we need to perform in a regulated method that can take into account the averages but allow for the exceptional.

A system, therefore, that will keep a continual rhythm to what you consider a workable approach, menu, and closing.

Orderly steps.

Most successful people and organizations do just that.

Hamburger chains order their food from the supplier, store it, prepare it when ordered, wrap it, slide it into a bag, and perhaps have you sign a waiver exempting them from prosecution at a later date. (Maybe not the best example, but I'm getting a little "piquish", here . . .)

Anyhow, I digress again. The point I am making is that there is a natural order, based on common sense in many cases, that get the process from 'A' to 'Z'. The approach in selling cars, or anything, is no different. In doing it over and over and over and over again, even the most inept of us will catch on. If you're successful as you go along, you will get better. You just have to.

Because . . . .

You're the BEST!

SELLING STEPS

In most organized dealerships, a training program is established to not only teach the salesperson how to sell their products but to guide them in the manner in which it is accomplished. On any team, be it sales or sports, working parts go together to create a favorable end result in an orderly and profitable manner. In other words, the left hand works a lot better when it knows what the right hand is doing. They can even determine when the foot becomes firmly ensconced in the mouth!

Training is typically presented to give everyone an idea as to what the business expects from its employees. Dress codes, schedules, work habits, benefits, pay, discussions of "drug free" environments and any and all work related areas will be usually covered in detail. All of these areas are fine and dandy, not to mention necessary, but the technique in which to further the business' success is what will be thoroughly gone over to keep the players all on the same page.

The techniques are commonly referred to as "Selling Steps." Different organizations use different methods but one will find that they usually incorporate the same ideas and habits in the whole package. Dealers may have anywhere from a "6 Step Method" to a "15 Step Method." They may vary in delivery but will usually be close in style in that they hope to simply "make the deal".

What I have done is to take a generic approach to the steps so that one could usually dovetail these into whichever system is implemented at your dealership or where you choose to work.

Step 1: Initial Greeting. Whether or not the buyer is a complete stranger as would be the case in a fresh 'up' or shares with you a degree of familiarity as in a scheduled appointment, the first contact makes a very strong and lasting impression. Remember, people are quick to make that overall judgement or opinion of anyone within seconds of meeting them. Think on your own experiences and recall how many times you made a binding decision based on a "gut" feeling. Good or bad, that is a fact, Grasshopper.

Make your introduction a sincere one. Meet your customer with a natural conviction that is neither pretentious or assuming. Shake hands as if you mean it. Gentlemen, bone crushing grips are not necessary! Also, since I did say "gentlemen", allow a lady to extend her hand first to shake. Otherwise, keep yours to yourself and just be your natural self. Some of you may have to "act" like some others who are more "natural", though. You know who you are!

If you are wearing sunglasses, remove them! People, consciously or subconsciously, make lasting impressions when eye to eye contact is made.

Pay attention to detail! How are they dressed? How many are in their party? Is the vehicle with them? Do they even *have* a vehicle?

You are establishing rapport! You are finding out what makes them tick! And you know that they are studying you right back. Keep your coffee, cigarette, cigar and otherwise bad breath at bay. You are in the limelight now. Step up!

It has been shown that most people forget names almost as quickly as they are given so it is a wonderful idea to write them down in your logbook as soon as they are given. By repeating their names as they're given, you are reinforcing them in your own mind. Ask them to spell their names for you. That helps, as well. Remember, the singular nicest word in any language is one's own name! Get it right! Establish their relationships with the others in the party. These are all oh so helpful in getting from point 'A' to point 'Z' as the deal progresses.

By the by, if that ketchup stain is still in your tie, change ties. Remove it. And clean your nails. If someone just gave you a wedgie, get it straight before you meet your clients! Tuck your shirt or blouse in and don't wear see-through clothing that may expose your bright orange thongs! (Boys AND girls.)

Now, if you didn't know already, ask your customer what brought him to the dealership.

Were they looking for new or used?

Automatic or 5 speed?

Two or four door?

I guess they would like air conditioning and a radio. True?

Perhaps they would like to save some time! (Who wouldn't?)"By getting just a little bit of information I can not only save time, but get the vehicle that is customized to your needs"!

"Follow me"!

Now, you have been professional, courteous, efficient to this point, and you may have even pointed out that it is much more comfortable in your office out of the sun, or wind, or rain, or the pigeon poop.

You have taken control of the situation because you are the PRO! This is what you do! You know the inventory (you've walked it daily, haven't you?) You know special programs. You want to garner information that is helpful to your customers. You want to help educate them by allowing them to share your own experiences and knowledge.

Now, after being escorted comfortably to your office, you can get some basic info to help your folks. I would like to point out that there are people with "challenged" credit histories that would immediately go to get pre-qualified because they already know where they stand. I am not saying that you should jump to any conclusions. In fact, there are a great many surprises in store for those who do assume.

Case in point, I was on a little fact finding mission is Scottsdale, AZ. I was pretty disgusting looking, in fact, after doing some engine work of my own. Deciding to take "advantage" of my appearance, (cut offs with holes, greasy hands, legs and fingernails, a billed cap that was partially torn, sneakers that the soles had partially detached themselves from the body) I proceeded to the dealership to check out some vans. After being approached by a salesman, I informed him that I was looking for something that had a little better tread than what I was using at the present (as I pointed to my "distressed" footwear). Again, I was on foot and he had probably seen me walk on to the lot.

Now, don't think I was just doing this to pull someone's chain. I wasn't. I really was interested in a van. I had been looking off and on for a while and I figured I would know the deal when I found it. Frankly, I was looking for a salesman!!!!!

Well, this was not the salesman I was in such high hopes of finding. After thoroughly checking me out from head to toe, he informed me that I was on private property and that if I wished to "dream" about a van, I could do it very well, thank you, from the public sidewalk 150 feet away.

"Thank you for your time", I said as I gently slithered back to my hole. Er, umh, the sidewalk, I mean.

Well, I was already out and ugly, so I proceeded next door. I walked through the lot and never did see anyone outside. It was about 112 degrees in the shade that day so I guess I didn't look "cool" enough to warrant a greeting from this place.

About this time, I decided to head on back home but it really was rather warm so I thought I would go to another dealership down the street where a friend of mine worked in the Finance Department. He'd give me a ride home, surely! It was early afternoon in the middle of the week and chances were that he would, or could, be free to give me a lift. Besides, I figured that with him being in Finance that I was hitting between one of the nine meals they usually experience daily! Just kidding, my producer friends!

So . . . walking there, I saw a van at yet *another* dealership that I could be interested in. I checked it out. Rather obviously, I thought. I walked around long enough to figure out the codes placed on the windshields that were used on their previously owned vehicles. I went back to the van. I walked around it. Although unlocked, it had a digital odometer so I couldn't check the mileage without the ignition switch on. I walked around some more.

Finally, a salesman approached me. "See anything you like?", he asked. I replied that I was interested in checking out the van and asked, like any customer, what was the price and the mileage. Remember, I was looking for a used van.

"The van is $19,995! Don't know the mileage . . . Wanna buy it"?

I answered with little enthusiasm with a shrug and a maybe, maybe not.

He handed me his card and said, "Give me a call when you can afford it. Have a nice day". He mumbles something under his breath as he turned from me to hurriedly get back to the confines of the A/C in the building.

Not to be deterred, because you see I *really* did want to get some input on the van. I wanted to know the mileage. I wanted to know how it drove. I wanted to smell it, feel it, check out the radio, a/c, cruise control. I was a buyer. I just needed to be sold the value in what I was buying.

I then noticed a salesman coming from a building next door and approached him. I asked if he would like to sell me "that van over there" since "Jim Bob" didn't want to.

Well, this guy did check me up and down, too. He did hesitate, I'll admit. But he did say he was going to get the keys so I could "scope out the scene."

Well, he was an OK salesman, I guess. I'll admit, I sold him to sell me since I really did think that the van would suit all of my needs. He offered me a test drive and of course, I accepted. I wouldn't buy the vehicle without checking it out. Would you?

Getting back to the dealership, he took me to his office and proceeded with his "system". It really wasn't much, to be honest, but at this point I figured the research would go to the brain stem and I would get this done so I could finally get the van I wanted. He did want to pull a credit bureau on me right away. I guess with the way I looked, I really couldn't accuse him of doing anything out of the ordinary (since I was not ordinary) but I just said that I would buy if we could come to an agreement on the deal. Further, if we were to come to that point, I knew that they would need my credit information.

I wasn't being stubborn, but in this game, like any others, it depends on whether one is pitching or catching. I'm not sure which is which, though.

We were so close to a deal that I knew it was done. At this point I allowed my credit to be pulled and was greeted by the desk manager at this point. I think they were pleasantly surprised to find my credit to be more than adequate. They probably thought it was 700 points higher than what they expected. Whatever . . . .

So, in a long winded fashion I just told you to never judge a book by its cover. Since this really did happen, though, I thought I would pass it along. My wife suggested that I approach that first dealership and make them a bargain by giving them a guaranteed training session for $25,000 or so to help them make more money. At the least, maybe they would hire and train a better sales staff in the future.

Cheap price to pay for such improved results!

So, getting back to the subject at hand, you have your customer in a comfortable situation, sitting comfortably, ready to save time and money. Please note that there are occasions where you are still on the lot and have to do the thinking on your feet. This method is just a little more conducive to helping the deal roll along a little smoother. In either scenario, the next step in moving along would be to gather some more information.

That is why we will call this:

Step 2: Fact Finding: The gathering of information.

At this stage, you will have already gathered a few bits of knowledge: what brought them to the dealership, were they here to see any person in particular (in the case of an 'Up'). You are advised to ask. They could either be logged from a day or two before with another salesperson or they could be an appointment. In either case, the best you could hope for would be a half deal even if you do all of the work and a sale is made. Besides, it's perhaps a moral and ethical approach to ask in advance. To do otherwise, you could be labeled as a 'Skater'. That is one who does a deal behind the backs of others by working appointments and such without doing the work on their own. It sounds so "Southern Cal", doesn't it? Skater, skater . . . .

So, having asked those previous questions, you will need a little bit more input to try to customize what your buyer will want or need. At this point, let's say they want a 4 door automatic with a/c and a radio. How many vehicles does your dealership have on the lot that fits that description? Quite a few, I would venture to guess. Now, you will want to know where their budget is desired. You notice I didn't say what they could *afford*! That is none of your business. We're talking very personal grounds here and you really don't want to go there.

Instead, let me emphasize the word 'budget'. You may ask where they have 'budgeted' their desired monthly payment. Let us say that they want to be around $300 a month. Okay, you might say. Further, you may ask if they currently have a payment on their current vehicle. Notice I didn't assume it to be a trade-in. They say yes, they do, and the payment is $300 a month. Typically, people want to stay around the budget they have been accustomed to. "Mr. and Mrs. Buyer", you ask, "just how much were you going to put down in cash"?

A usual answer would be little or nothing.

You just say "Great"!

"Now", you may ask, "are you considering trading in your current vehicle?" They may say yes, they may say no (buyers sometimes don't like to tip their hands . . . I mean, if you know too much you might be able to make a deal! As such, they really do want to trade but figure that is a separate negotiation altogether), or they might say maybe. You let them know that either way is just dandy! You will give them a price with and without their vehicle as a trade!

You now would like to know if there are any liens on the vehicle; in other words, is there a payoff to a lender that is holding the vehicle as collateral. So, yes, they have a balance of $5,000 owed to 1st National Bank of Wizenheim and it would have to be satisfied if the vehicle was traded in.

A very simple equation may be used to determine monthly payments to dollars. Even in the days of 0% or 1.9% loans, err on the high side. You can always make it better but you want to cover yourself.

Consider each $1,000 financed to equal $25 to $30 a month in payment. I know this is on the high side but remember you don't have any credit information on them at this point so it could only get better if they have great credit. If their credit is in the figurative toilet, you won't be giving them false hopes.

So, let's say you're guessing their car is worth $4,000 wholesale. That's the true value: the price that the car will bring at a wholesale auction. With a little time you may get pretty good at guessing but again, err on the safe side and figure low in this case. So with $5,000 owed on a car that is worth $4,000, that shows the vehicle is "out of equity" or "upside down". With $1,000 cash and their trade they would be even with $0 owed to their current lien-holder.

So, with $0 down and figuring $30 per month per $1,000 owed, there is $30 dollars a month out of their budget of $300 leaving a payment of $270. Or $9,000 financed (still using a $30 payment per $1,000 of the note).

Figuring around 10% for tax, title and license on a $9K car, let's just ball park the amount and figure it to be around $1,000.

So, there goes another $30 leaving $240 a month for a car.

Dividing the $240 by $30 gives eight times or eight times $1,000 is their budget for a car. Using my fancy 'HP', that comes to $8,000. ('HP' is Hewlett-Packard for you non-Geeks.)

So, you have been told by the buyer that what they wanted was a 4 door automatic with air conditioning and a radio. They want their payment to be around $300 a month. They want to trade their car in and pay off the balance.

Figuring all of that in there, you are going to take them to a car that sells for $8,000. If you wish to deal without their trade, you'll find a vehicle, I'm sure, around the $9,000 range.

So now you're moving on. You are not negotiating a daggone thing here. I repeat, you are just getting what they expect in their new vehicle and how much they would be paying for it.

You have helped bring reality to the table down the road a piece and you have just laid the groundwork for "step selling".

Hold on, 'Step Selling' is coming uno momento: just a little further in this here pages . . . .

Remember that you are gathering facts. You are not selling options. You are trying to make this deal simple and overcome any walls that the buyer is placing in front of the deal.

K.I.S.S.

Keep It Simple, Stupid.

That is just what we are doing.

You will not ask questions such as the following. They will just make your deal harder or make it not happen at all.

Examples:

What color would you like?
What do you think your trade is worth?
Would you like to drive the car? (Duh!)
Do you like the moon roof on your vehicle?
Would you like a leather interior?

On and on. I guess you can see the point I am trying to make. Don't limit your options. Believe me when I tell you that they will tell you all that they want. And soon!

That moon roof will be $30 a month by itself. The leather could be the same. And you should know the law: whatever color the buyer would want would be the one that you do not have in stock! (They're all black at night, remember?)

You are just going to show them, without doing anything but agreeing with them, what their money will buy with the parameters they gave you to deal with.

Now, before taking them to the lot to show them the vehicle (or bringing it to them while they wait in your comfortable office), you will need to get some information on their vehicle in the event that it is used as a trade.

Step 3: Get the **Trade Evaluated.** There is a form used at the dealership that will cover a variety of items related to the vehicle. It will have an area for the Vehicle Identification Number or a.k.a. V.I.N.

It will ask the mileage of the vehicle.

There are check off spaces for most of the major components and an area to make additional notes.

Since you are such a prepared sales person, you will have one of these forms handy at all times. Requesting a hand from your customer, you ask for help in getting the info on their vehicle. I have found that if you get the buyer involved that it is a more pleasant and faster experience. For instance, have the buyer read off the mileage or V.I.N. to you. Remember that you are responsible for this information so verify it later. For that time though, you are teammates, ain't ya?

Now, let's take a spin, shall we? Invite the customer to allow you to go for a drive in their car. You can get a general feel for the condition but more importantly, the buyer will psychologically be the seller! You will hear what a great, or perhaps crappy, car this is, but you will be learning some of the "buttons" that make this buyer tick. There may be options that are lacking on the trade that you find are important to the deal. You may notice the brakes are "steel on steel". The air conditioning may be going on the blink.

It is advised that you do an inspection as if you were the one buying the trade personally. This will let you know the good, bad and the ugly about the trade as well as its finer points. Those with even basic mechanical skills will do just fine but for those with no experience in engines and mechanics, it would not be a bad idea to get some pointers from someone in the know.

A basic walk around of the vehicle is suggested in the evaluation. Pop the hood and check for obvious defects. Pull out the dipstick and check for metal filings or oil that is way past due for changing. The belts may show cracking. There may be evidence of fluid leaks around the various enclosures of the engine and drive train.

Inspect the tires for wear. Generally, if the remaining tread covers at least to Lincoln's head on a penny it is adequate. Just barely, but it would avoid deducting an additional $100 or so per tire.

Check the U-joints on front wheel drive cars for evidence of lubrication leakage. That could further the cost of repair at $350 to $500.

Obviously, dents, dings and windshield pits and cracks should be noted. Fading paint is another deduction.

Observe closely for paint overspray on the rubber gaskets around the windows and roof areas. This could indicate a prior accident and could greatly drop the value of the car.

Inspect the trunk area. Is there a good spare? Are the tools (jack, lug wrench, etc.) still in storage?

Is it cleaned out?

Is the glove compartment cleaned out?

The last two are indications that the buyer is ready to trade and move up to a new car! Make mental notes on all of the above in addition to what you mark down on your evaluation form.

Yes, this could really be a vehicle that comes under the category of not "what's it worth?" but rather "what's it weigh?". As in scrap. Crushed. Junk.

$500. Top price.

Or it could be a wonderful, low mileage trade that you know will bring even more in value to the table. In any case, you're establishing a relationship and learning a little more what it like in the buyer's shoes. You're getting closer to a deal already!

Now, take it for a drive around the block or so with the buyer along with you. Remember, this is the buyer's comfort zone and this time together will greatly assist you further in the establishing of a "buying" relationship. Return to the dealership, complete the trade evaluation form and continue the process of selling in steps.

This next step could be called a steppe or a sub step but it is an important one. Move on to . . . .

Step 4: Step Selling.

We have been leading to this step. Previously, you were given the parameters by the buyer and you are doing what they have asked of you. To get the vehicle they wanted for the budget they, themselves, supplied. Look, I do know that reality has all kinds of circumstances and there are those of you who are reading this and are saying, "Right! Like, really, Dude, there isn't going to be anyone who is going to fall for this crap".

First, it is not a misleading adventure I am after. I do know that some folks are going to ask for the Spitshoot 144 Sportster and will expect you to get it for them. Fine! Just adapt to the situation. It is still a matter of budget and payment and cutting to the quick. It works! Not only in cars, but in life.

If you want a $500,000 house with $0 down, simple math and a finite lifetime dictate your payments will be higher than the $750 a month payment that your budget allows. This is an example of using common sense and eliminating the bull doodoo by asking for their own conditions that you are being asked to follow.

So, you take them to the vehicle that best fits the conditions that were given by them! I'll repeat: the buyer set the conditions.

The conditions happened to dictate an exceptionally valued four door automatic with a radio, air conditioning and is priced from $8,000 to $9,000.

If it is the Spitshoot 144 Sportster you may just have a done deal!

However, assuming that it is not that spiffy example of over the road craftsmanship, the buyer may just look at you with more than a little malice.

Be aware, my loquacious desert dwellers in Arizona, that carrying a concealed weapon can be legal. (Customers could be carrying!) Be sure your rapport was greatly enforced in the previous steps!

Now, moving right ahead, you may be made aware by the buyer that a moon roof was a necessity; that the vehicle being shown wasn't brand new; that he absolutely *needed* an eight disc CD changer!

"Well", you reply, "I was merely trying to listen to you when you informed me of the budget you had set. If you need the vehicle that you are now suggesting (the buyer has pointed this out by now or made strong suggestions), I'll be glad in assisting you with helping you purchase it. It is a little more than what you led me to believe you wanted to spend, but . . . let's go! It's your money!"

Now, the buyer himself has set a higher figure to deal with. He just told you! And remember, you have no need to sell the first $300 a month or the first $9,000: that much the buyer has already sold himself!

You may start to focus on presenting the value of the difference that is needed to consummate the deal.

It's the buyer's money, after all . . . .

Step 5: Sell Current Inventory.

You are self employed. Right? Well, in a sense. You are not on some government payroll that will pay you regardless of performance. You are on an incentive plan that the dealership so wisely set up just for you.

It's called: work or starve! That's being self employed. The more you put in, the more you will get out. The better and smarter you become in applying your time and effort the more consistent your results and thus income will be.

But . . . there is a little bit of difference from truly being self-employed. Chances are you will get a W-2 form. Additionally, there is a very large difference in that you didn't have to go to Hip National to stock the inventory. You didn't have to buy or lease the property that it all sits on. You don't have to pay the real estate taxes or the electrical bills. There is no upkeep to be concerned with.

There is a great amount that has been invested by the powers that be. Those powers that be are the ones who sign your pay vouchers.

They are the ones who try to anticipate a market *before* it arrives. Huge sums are spent for all types of marketing.

This is all to hopefully sell what they so wisely put on the property for you "self employed" (self motivated) Whiz Kids to move and make a profit with.

They are very concerned and lovely folks, those powers that be.

Always thinking just of you!

The very least you could do in return is to free up their investments so they can do it all over again. Great plan! It works!

You are not a broker. You are not sitting just anywhere. You are at the place of business where you can not only get very close, if not exactly, what the customer wants or needs, but you have the additional advantage of actually being a salesperson that can sell what you have on hand.

That is the reason you surely must take advantage of the opportunity that has been given to you. Remember, there are orders all of the time that are canceled before the customer takes delivery.

If you weren't sure, that is no sale. You don't get paid. Disneyland, world and universe will all have to wait.

Your honey will be oh so disappointed!

But!

If the buyer takes delivery and you have done your job properly, a deal is consummated! You get a voucher!

You, too, may wear a hat with big floppy ears!

All because the powers that be really wanted you and your family to have fun on vacation! Again, I can't tell you emphatically enough just how sweet those PTB be.

(Powers That Be)

Love abounds when everyone sells cars, has fun and makes money.

So, very simply, sell what you have on hand. It makes life a whole lot simpler and gives you time to move on to the next mountain!

Step 6: Present the Vehicle.

After you have learned from the customer that he may want a little more than what you had initially offered; and even if he has told you he definitely wants certain options, it's a good idea to still take him to a more base model of the vehicle he desires. You want to make a point of selling the value in a lesser priced vehicle in the event that the buyer cannot financially swing as much in a purchase as he, or even you, thought. This is a backup so NEVER put down a vehicle's qualities after you think that a more equipped vehicle is going to be bought. You could just talk yourself out of a deal completely.

Now you will locate the vehicle that will fit the wants and needs of the buyer. After mutual agreement on which one it is, you will take the time to get into the vehicle and pull it away from the line. Leave the engine running (unless there are rules against it at your place of work). Also, release the trunk to prepare for when you will be showing the rear of the vehicle. You want to show this vehicle as apart from the masses and, in effect, you are making it a little more exclusive.

Take a short little walk around the vehicle yourself just to make sure that everything is quite up to snuff. It has happened that lot attendants, sales staff, even other demo's could have placed a scratch or a ding on it and even if the customer bought that vehicle, it would affect your check since the repairs would be added to the overall cost, lessening the profit margin. Besides, it shows the buyer you are looking out for his best interest.

Injecting a note here: product knowledge is something that cannot be overstated! It shows professionalism. It shows the character of someone who wants to be at the top of their game.

For you, the salesperson, it breeds overwhelming confidence.

People do business with professionals. People want to deal with the best representatives that they can. People can detect bull doodoo when listening to a presentation.

So, take the time to learn about all of your products. It is never ending since they are ever changing. Subscribe to trade magazines like "Car and Driver" or "Motor Trend", to name a couple. The car manufacturers typically have publications that are sent regularly to your dealership. Read them!

The manufacturers also have training that rewards the sales people with certification relating to product knowledge and customer satisfaction.

It all goes hand in hand, you see.

So, for the presentation, you are indeed knowledgeable. That is what I will take for granted or you would not have read this far already. What I am going to present to you is an example of a basic walk around without going into the fine detail. Detailed demonstrations are better left to an experienced trainer from your dealership that could show you the finer points related to your products. What I will do, however, is to point out a few points that may set you apart from the crowd.

Just like you did when you pulled the car out of the line . . . .

Starting at the drivers door and going clockwise as you did in the trade evaluation, point out the examples of *Safety* the vehicle has to offer. That could be steel side door guard beams, crumple zones in the fenders and hood areas, independent strut suspension (control of a vehicle makes it a safe vehicle: O. J. Simpson had a LOT of control in his Bronco after the fact); since you release the hood before exiting the vehicle, open the hood fully and point out the collapsible steering column; breakaway engine mounts that direct the engine in a direction downward rather than into the passengers' area; the halogen headlamps (or argon, or laser rays, whatever) that brightens the depths of night into a Spring day at noon; make notice of the new state of the art bumper system available.

You will make a point of showing how to service the fluids of the engine area and just how convenient all of the reservoirs and dipsticks are placed. Remove the air filter to show that you, too, can be a shade tree mechanic!

Now, you may want to speak of *Performance*. You may want to bring up the stats on how fast the car can do from 0-60 MPH. Perhaps something particular about the drive train in general would be what you think the buyer would like to hear. You may want to point out the handling characteristics and control with the Anti-Lock Braking system. The rack and pinion steering is made for reactions that seem you only have to think of before the car reacts! I am getting excited!

In a well designed engine, I have used good, new nickels to demonstrate how smoothly an engine can run. With the engine idling, place the nickel on edge on a flat, level section of the engine and point out how it still stands. Impressive!

Seriously, though, use extreme caution: the engine must be running, of course, for this demonstration and items like neckties and necklaces could be very dangerous around moving engine parts.

If you *really* want to give a show, carefully move the throttle lever ahead to 'rev' the engine. Doing it gradually, the nickel continues to stand! You may have to shield it from the cooling fan, however, to keep the wind from blowing the nickel down.

This has never failed to be an impressive demonstration.

It is also one I could never use when I started with the Yugo Car Sales Inc,. LTD, dealership.

I did use the nickel to buy one later, though!

The *Economy* of a vehicle is another hot button in these days (they have always been these days) of high fuel costs. Know the city/highway figures on this vehicle and point out the difference from 5-speed to the automatic. You may have to put them in a car with a manual transmission and could use this as perhaps a justification.

Perhaps the vehicle has spark plugs that go 100,000 miles before changing. Point out the lack of breaking in period. Mention how the paint, plastics and metals have been tested in the extremes of both hot and cold at specialized testing grounds at different locations in the country. It is very good economy not to have to replace items in the vehicle for many years and that's what these time consuming tests have proven. Additionally, this all helps to retain future resale value in the vehicle.

Moving along to the passenger side of the vehicle, point out the exceptional finish on the car. Mention the particular process, perhaps, about the "ionization" process used that electronically bonds the high tech primer to the various alloys that make up the framework and platform of the vehicle. Speak of the multiple layers involved to create such a magnificent reflection. Stroke it as you would the finest silk and indicate the lushness of it.

I have even known a salesman who encouraged his buyer to lick the finish to show how smooth it was. He happened to be explaining the "Desert Protection Package" at the time which is popular in the Southwest to further protect the finish.

By the way, selling add-ons increases the gross profit. Did I mention that?

Also, that salesman's customer did buy the car. That just proves a "smooth tongue" can make the deal!

Point out the aerodynamic styling of the roof line that decreases the drag coefficiency of the vehicle. Show how the windshield may be slightly recessed at the support on the side to discourage rainwater or windshield washer fluid from sneaking in through an open window.

Open the door and actually hang on it! Show just how well made this product is! You're entertaining as well as knowledgeable, huh?

In a four door vehicle, approach the back door, open it, and invite the buyer to try the great roominess afforded. Point out the split back seats or console. Show the rear air vent. Demonstrate the child proof safety latches (new sales people: beware! In training, the "old" pros always do this to "greenpeas" only to make them escape by climbing to the front of the vehicle to get out).

Continuing with the demonstration of the fold down seats, move to the rear of the car to open the trunk. Show just how handy and spacious the area in the trunk is. Relate the size to something the buyer can relate to: a large Thermos cooler, skis, groceries, etc. Jump in it yourself. If so equipped, with a little practice beforehand you can have the trunk shut while you are inside and use the safety release to demonstrate the emergency exit feature.

We have all heard horror stories about youngsters who were trapped in refrigerators as well as trunks. Show the buyer how it operates and how a potential tragedy may be avoided.

Show where the emergency equipment is located. If you *really* want to show off, change the tire! It takes but a few minutes and is something no salesperson anywhere has cared enough to show. A buyer with limited mechanical skills truly appreciates this.

Point out how *Durable* the vehicle is by some well placed thumps on the rear bumper. Jump up and down in the trunk.

Heck, if you can, pick up the rear of the vehicle a foot or so and let it drop. The buyer may just buy on the spot out of pure fear!

Okay . . . back to reality . . . .

Now, continue around back to the driver's door. Invite your buyer to take a seat and position the seat settings to where they are the most comfortable. Point out the ease of which all of the controls are in reach. Make a general explanation of the controls at this point and at the appropriate moment (thinking on your feet as you do, you will know. I am talking just a few minutes, at best, here) invite the buyer to have seat in the passenger's side. As he gets up to do this, it is the opportune time to ask for his driver's license. It is ALWAYS the case to get a copy of the driver's license to leave with the dealership management. This is not only for the sale; it is for your personal safety. It's nice for management to know the stranger with whom you've left the dealership.

After logging in (with your manager) the information of who you are with and which car you are taking, YOU drive off of the lot. There are a number of reasons for you personally driving. First, you are in control of the situation. You know the area both on the dealership lot as well as the local streets. You have experience with the controls of the vehicle.

And you are back to demonstrating how wonderful life can be in this new and wonderful replacement to the horse.

That is why you are now on

Step 7: Demonstration.

Depending on the type of vehicle you are demonstrating, you should have a pre-arranged route that you are to follow. For example, a compact vehicle would do well in maneuvering parking lots as well as streets and highways; an off road vehicle could be shown at its finest in as area where all wheel drive could scream out and shout, "I am the MAN! Do NOT be messing with ME!"

That's what they say when they are climbing hills and gullies. Who knew?

A luxury vehicle could show its performance and quiet ride in an otherwise noisy environment on a major highway system. You get the idea.

But before you really get out on the drive, stop at an appropriate spot that will show off the vehicle as you change positions with the buyer. He has had a little bit of time to watch you use the controls and has acclimated to a point. Relaxation. Getting a little bit used to the situation.

Pull the vehicle where a lake or beautiful landscaping is in the background. When you are changing seats, take a moment and invite the buyer to take a look at the vehicle all over again. It should be looking really *sweet! Appearance!*

In taking the seats with the buyer now driving, refresh his memory with all of the control features. Point out how much you like the cruise control as you're taking off. How it feels just fine to slip out of those hot, cramped shoes and "crinkle" your toes.

Use 'Action' verbs and phrases that are exciting, give feeling, give a sense of authority and, dare I say, present a *destiny!*

There are times to just be quiet. You may be approaching that even now as the buyer is soaking it all up. He is aware of the controls. He is trying them out. Let him! After a while, you might want to let him know just how much *Comfort* you're experiencing while just going along for the ride.

After a bit, a few trial closes could be thrown out there. You know, like: "What do you think your neighbors will think when they see this parked in your driveway"?

Or: "Your boss won't be jealous when she sees this and cut your pay, will she"?

How about: "Your wife (or husband) will probably take this car right over and make you use your other one. As soon as the other car is out of the shop, that is".

Trial closes get reactions. 'Yes's' and 'no's'. 'Maybe's' and 'maybe not's'. But you are learning the way the wind is blowing and can take remedies to go in the right direction. The majority of the time, if the buyer is "carred up" right, you are going to be getting positive feedback and helping the buyer to take more of a possession in his mind.

Acceptance is half of the battle!

Arriving back at the dealership, have the buyer pull the vehicle into the 'Sold' line. This can be a real area, but anywhere you can see a spot to pull into can be your own personal 'Sold' line.

As a real pro, again, you have your 'Sold' sticker in your belongings that you write the stock number on and have the buyer initial. Place the sticker under the windshield wiper. That way, no other person will be buying his vehicle out from under him.

And you know if you may have deal or not. An acceptance has taken place!

Get the information off of the vehicle at this point. Have the buyer assist you, if you want. You're a team, remember?

Get the V.I.N. Get the mileage. Get the stock number. Get a list of the features of the vehicle from the sticker. Write the M.S.R.P. (manufacturer's suggested retail price) or the price listed by the dealership which would include the dealer installed options.

Smile pleasantly and have your buyer follow. You're about to show just how easy it is to do business with you and your associates!

"Take and Break and Relax!"

Well, that is kinda, sorta the next step. A comfortable and reassuring time for both you and the buyer is at hand. But that is not the point. I am talking to you. I want you to just cool it for a few moments and relax.

There has been just a little too much in the way of regimentation leading up to now. Well, since Org and Tumba, anyway. It's been getting a little too dry for my own tastes so I figured I didn't want to be too much of a hypocrite by asking you to do as I say and not as I do.

I guess, since you've put your feet up and are starting to doze a little, you wouldn't mind a little story. Really short. Honest!

This has nothing to do with sales as such. It has everything to do with sales.

???????

Well, it's true and it's relaxing. Just keep quiet and listen. *Please?*

Poochie and Geetie

1961 was not necessarily a simpler time to those who lived then. There were still the same worries with the family budget, who "begat" who; school yard bullies existed to torment the more frail amongst us.

J.F.K. was the Chief Executive. The French were alone in their paradox known as Viet Nam. Goldie Hahn was a teenager in Suitland, Md. Slicked back hair and ducktails. Poodle skirts. And Poochie and Geetie were twins.

They were in their 50's, if I were to guess. I'm not sure, since I was a youngster of 8 or 9 years old. (Doing the math, aintcha? I'm 51, now.) They had worked for my great grandfather and continued on working with my great uncles in doing work around the farm as well as being employed as well drillers.

Around 5'10" with sinewy bodies the color of the desert floor at sunrise, they were extremely hard workers with more than a little gusto when the weekend approached. They looked forward to the time when they could "carry on", as they put it. As Friday rolled around, they could go until the wee hours with drinking contests that included holding two quarts of beer to their mouths simultaneously with the loser buying the next four quarts. People would always stop and gape at the spectacle.

I had known Poochie and Geetie my whole life and there wasn't anything abnormal in their habits or their appearances. They were Poochie and Geetie and that's just who they were and they did what they did. Although not identical twins, people could occasionally confuse them unless they remembered that Poochie was toothless and had a terrific craving for mustard whose stains on his shirt gave him away. A little wealthier, Geetie had several teeth remaining.

Although not educated in a formal sense, both brothers were held with regard when it came to their duties and abilities as untiring workers. I was one who could recognize that it would take more than a few quarts of beer (2 at a time) to keep them from whatever work was ahead of them.

Working for Uncle Gilbert and Uncle Taylor, Saturdays were usually a little bit laid back. You *were* expected to show, however, even if it was but for half a day. Uncle Gilbert was known for his Saturday hot dog eating contests for which he would put up a prize. There would be weight lifting contests with bar bells made from a forge usually reserved for drawing out bits used in drilling wells. All in all, it was a day for making a few easy dollars and to promote camaraderie. Of course, the hot dogs kept me coming. And it was as if we were all family: black and white.

So, it was a Saturday after Poochie and Geetie had drawn a tie with their beer guzzling contest from the night before. They were ready to work, and did.

Now, my uncles had some livestock and most everyone had a chore or two to do in that area, too, as long as you were being paid for doing something.

Seeing Poochie and Geetie's lack of focus, Uncle Gilbert gave them both some very simple tasks to perform. One happened to be what seemed to be as simple as it could be: get the recently weaned calf back inside the outbuilding so some fencing could be repaired. They didn't even have to do the fencing. Just get the calf penned!

Well, I happened by when Poochie and Geetie were pretty relieved at such a simple chore. Do it and they'd be gone!

The calf was not that large. A nine (or eight) years old boy's guess would be around 350 pounds. A calf. A baby. Maybe 250 pounds . . . Don't know . . . Not sure . . .

But it *was* stronger than Poochie and Geetie.

Pores exuding the fruits of their labors of the night before, they shoved, they pushed, they whipped with straps, they cussed, and, given a little more time, I think they may have even bit the itty bitty baby cow on the butkus.

The calf dug in and would not budge.

Off to the side, their coworkers were in stitches and taking side bets on who would be kicked first.

Poochie and Geetie were my pals, though. I thought it to be a little humorous, I have to admit, but I really had to help them out. Of course, when I did offer, the others thought that really funny, too. That's what the situation needed: another clown so they egged me on, as well.

Well, I hadn't been big enough to be in their beer contest the night before and I certainly wasn't half the man they were, so I had to do what I thought would work. I wasn't that strong; I was limited in my resources!

Going into the shed, I scooped a handful of milk substitute used in the formula made for weaning calves. I made a bit of a paste and walking up to it, I smeared a little on the calf's nose.

That was some really good stuff, don't ya know! Well, it followed me right along into the shed. Docile, it was. Happy, too! Poochie and Geetie looked at each other and then turned their smiles to me. I felt pretty cool: the rights of manhood or something. Remember the year. It was simpler then. Maybe I lied a bit at the start of the story.

I do know one reason I have recalled that story and lost others to "Sometimers Disease": it showed, as Uncle Gilbert used to love to say, that "brains wins again".

I heard he said that when he heard the tale.

I remember thinking it was easier to lead something with a good idea than it was trying to push something into something they weren't sure of. Didn't get kicked or bit, either!

It's now 2004 and it still works.

Relaxed yet?

Good. 'Cuz story time's over. Sweet, 'weren't' it?

And since you are relaxed and I'm breaking up the steps to meander a little, let me point out what you may have noticed with some italicized words I injected in Steps 1-7.

Safety
Performance
Appearance
Comfort
Economy
Durability

Now, don't get *SPACED* out . . . .

These are known as some of the more common "hot buttons". Depending on your buyer, there will be at least one of these areas that need to be stressed in the overall selling process.

For instance, parents searching for a car for their school aged child would be undoubtedly looking for a car that was safe, economical and durable.

If the child was with them, he or she would certainly not care about those as much and would be looking for how cool it would look and how it would handle.

Having parents and child together may put you to task to try to please both but it is done all of the time. Just remember who is signing the check. 51% of the sale should go that way. Or, of course, to the woman who always influences the decision . . . whatever . . . .

When you are first meeting with your buyers, you may even be advised to ask what their highest priorities in a vehicle are. As you're presenting the vehicle, keep those items at the front of your mind and sell accordingly.

The young men (I wouldn't insult a lady with this remark!) would do well this Saturday night to remember in approaching a nice young lady which of these buttons are more important to them: Safety (is she wearing a brass knuckle stud in her left nostril?), Performance (without the right meeting and greeting, you may never know!), Appearance (look, but don't touch!), Comfort (again, you may never know!), Economy ("Hey, Sweet Cheeks, how about buying Ol' Dad a drink?" I doubt that would work well. Yea, that would be economical, though.), or Durability ("Excuse me, Miss: can you bear how overbearing I am with my halitosis that's destined to be in the Mayo Clinic Hall of Fame?")

Relaxed AND Spaced. What a swell time we're having!

I guess we should get back to these steps, shall we?

Step 8: Relax and Regroup.

So, you've had a pretty encouraging time with the buyer by this time. You have properly 'carred' up the buyer, good rapport is established, you haven't let any fender trading get in the way of the deal ("She sure is a beaut, ain't she? Ready to buy it?")

You have set a good foundation with this relationship and established good, sound walls to help complete the structure with:

1) Started with a sincere introduction.
2) You have shown confidence through experience and product knowledge.
3) You have presented evidence of good work ethics. Although you have given the buyer "hope for gain" in this deal, you have made a point of 'under promising' and 'over delivering'.
4) An exhibition of excitement has been evident. You have entertained. You have shown the buyer's combined benefits of doing business with you and your dealership in a believable fashion.

Now, in short order, you'll be putting the roof to the walls and foundation which you've built.

I do want to stress, however, the Close could come at any time! With experience, you will know just when that time is.

With the steps done in order, you will be amazed at just how much your work and devotion are appreciated by the buyer.

But for now, you are in a relaxing mode. This is the time to get the buyer off of his feet and just sit him (again, her, them, etc. may all be inserted. I don't want anyone to think I am anything BUT politically correct!) on his butt and get a drink of his choice: coffee, soft drink, water, or whatever is in the dealership.

You want to just unwind for a few moments and allow the air to freshen, so to speak. Talk about the weather, the local football team, his job, whatever, but get off of the buying process for just a little bit. Not *too* long, but just enough to RELAX both him and you.

This is also a time for you to mentally break away a bit from being too close to him. I know this may seem a little bit contradictory, but it is a necessary function to remember that this is a business and you are there to not only get your buyer what he needs but you owe it to the dealership to make a reasonable profit on the transaction. It is quite a bit easier when you are not too emotionally involved.

So, you've had a nice little chat. You've sipped a little brew. You recall that you have a car deal that needs doing!

So now . . . it is time to

Step 9: Write up the Deal.

Standard paperwork at your dealership will have what is in effect a "bargaining form". In some circles it may be referred to as a "4 Square". Otherwise, it is the paperwork that is done to hash out the deal.

Typically, it is standard to list all of the information from both the vehicle being purchased as well as the trade information, if applicable. This would include the Stock number, make, model, trim level, any accessories installed by the manufacturer or the dealership, etc.

In an area devoted to the new vehicle, list the items included in the package. Cruise control, 4 speed automatic transmission, power windows and door locks, tilt wheel, ABS, CD player, Bose system, . . . whatever.

You really want to reinforce all of the value in what the buyer came in to replace his vehicle with.

On the other hand, it is time to point out in the Trade area of the paperwork how many miles the trade has (out of warranty), the nicks and bumps, the worn tires, the questionable braking system, faded paint, metal filings evidenced in the oil on the dipstick, etc.

You are obviously pointing out the very reason the buyer came in to purchase. The buyer's other vehicle is not going to work for this person's needs for long and a solution is needed for that very problem.

Fill the form out completely. It remains a record of the deal for the file even after all is said and done. But the main reason is to create a synopsis of all that has happened in the selling process to this point.

Cliff Notes does it! Reader's Digest does it! So do you!

You are condensing the entire experience to this point and bringing the Value of the deal to the forefront!

An old car dealer has passed down the saying, "Sell on your feet; Negotiate on your seat!"

An even older car dealer reminded him that whenever one negotiates, money is lost!

(That leaves one to ponder: "why are Wisemen and wiseguys opposites?" . . . .)

So, remember the selling price set by the dealer is the selling price. Not hard to remember. Keep that in mind and believe it! If you have done your job so far, don't even have a concern. Remember that million you have in the bank. You're not stressed: you're rich!

Believe!

Deal from strength!

Alrighty . . . now that you have a form all filled out and you're just busting with pride of your penmanship, it is now time to get some numbers. Since you are not an expert used car buyer and don't have the computer in your hip pocket to access, you need to get the dealer's selling price. It will be the same as the car was listed on the lot, but the desk manager will give a complete scenario just for you!

So, the next step is

Step 10: Get the Numbers.

In this instance, you will be supplied with not only the gross figures, but you will be given monthly payments, as well. As most buyers look at what their budget can afford, this is a logical approach.

This step will vary with different dealers. For instance, some would have the salesperson bring the paperwork to the desk and the desk manager would fill out the numbers.

Some would have the salesperson call the desk to receive the figures over the phone without ever leaving the buyer.

Of course, there are variations but the obvious holds true: you now have real numbers on a real deal to work with. You have the selling price, trade in value allowed, monthly payments offered with a suggested down payment to make it work so well.

Who knew it could be so easy?

Moving right along, we come to

Step 11: Negotiate.

I know I said somebody said when you negotiate you lose money. I know. I know. But the fact of the matter is that you still have to "customize" the financial end for your buyer. Don't you?

For instance, your manager may have given you numbers along the line of :

Down payment:	$4,500-$4,800.
Monthly payment:	$465-$490
Trade Value:	$5,200-$5,500
Selling price of vehicle:	$21,489.00

Now, as you will be individually trained by your respective dealership, I won't go into an exact means of presenting the numbers. What I will do, yet again, is give the basic presentation.

Remember that these are the true and exact numbers given to you by the "Powers That Be" albeit a range is shown until details are fine-tuned. Accordingly, they are just and proper. They have all of the information at their disposal and are merely passing on what they themselves have. Your mission, should you decide to accept, is to present them in a sincere and convincing manner.

A typical presentation could go like this:

You would turn the paperwork so the buyers could see it well as you "read" it upside down and refer to the appropriate section.

"Mr. and Mrs. Buyer, the selling price of your vehicle, equipped as you like it, is $21,489. Based on today's market value in the "Phoenix" area, your 'trade' is valued in the area of $5,200 to $5,500!

"With only $4,500 to $4,800 down, my manager says we can keep your monthly payment at only $465 to $490!"

Now, "ferme la bouche!"

(Maitenant, "shut your mouth".)

Just listen and watch. It's tough, but then, so are you! Wait . . . and wait some more. "He who speaks first . . ."; well, anyway, let's just say the upper hand goes to Mr. or Ms. 'Quiety'.

The buyer speaks (since you didn't).

Quite often, the response from the buyer will be something along the line of "That's too much!"

Well, don't assume anything. You have to fact-find. This is easily done, in fact. Your response should be along the lines of, "What is too much?"

Mr. and Mrs. Buyer might say that it's the whole thing. They may say that it is the price of the car. They may say it's the monthly payment.

They may say it's too much info all at once.

Who knows?

Just don't assume anything. I have seen where their attention has really been on the monthly payment all along and it's the high down stroke (a.k.a. down payment) that's freaking them out.

That is the reason you ask. Let them tell you. If it is the down payment, perhaps the deal can be adjusted to better suit their needs.

Perhaps their objection is to the "low" price of their trade. Again, perhaps the deal can be adjusted to better suit their needs.

There are ways to make the deal work. Your job is to mix profit with satisfaction. In negotiating the deal, there a quite a few methods to get from point 'A' to point 'B'. Sometimes, they are called closes.

I prefer to think of it as common sense with a dab of experience.

Maybe the payment is perceived as too high. Well, with less money financed, we can mathematically reduce the payments, right? Perhaps they could qualify for a "short term" 72 month loan rather than a longer one at 84 or 96 months!

Perhaps they may want to hold on to the trade. If it is worth less than what is owed, it's rolling a debt into the deal and making the monthly payment more.

But, that's maybe not what they want. It's your job to string all of it together. In a bit, we'll go over a number of closes and how they can be applied but for now, let's just cruise along with no major objections or boogaboos in this transaction.

So, let's say that the buyer said that the down payment was too high. Well, for that matter, so was the monthly.

And you know, the trade could be more, couldn't it?

Taking each item, one at a time, commit your buyer to what *they will do*!

Unless the buyer is paying cash, the purchase price is insignificant. It will come up and be what it is. Regardless of the amount paid, it all comes down to how much is being financed.

So, after using the closes you haven't learned yet, you have the buyer tell you that with $1,000 cash and the trade, a deal could happen if the payment is kept to a range of $375-$390. The trade is still in the deal and the lien on it would be paid in full.

Alrighty, then. You may not be able to do it, but you owe it to your buyer to give it a fighting chance.

Simply condense it, as above, and have them give their "OK" by initialing the statement. Get the cash, check or credit card for the $1,000. That's the offer so you're helping to extend it. Earnest money! Just like buying a house. No offer is entertained until a little scratch backs up the mouth.

The difference is that if the deal doesn't happen, there is no loss of money. But hey . . . nothing ventured, nothing gained!

To this point, you have a commitment. You have cash. That too, has another name: "glue". It helps hold the deal together so you can help. It will happen!

Next, since there is financing, a credit history is required. Better known as the credit bureau.

Take a complete application from the buyer. It will ask what all lenders need to know: name, address, home owner or not, time at the address, age, dependents, social security number, phone number, job, how long there, address of employer, etc.

Make you application in a neat and orderly fashion. When the deal is done, you'd be surprised how many marginal loans are TD'd (turned down) because of just plain sloppiness and lack of information.

I know sometimes the buyer can be in a hurry, but let them know that's why you're doing this right at this time: to save them time down the road. It's more quickly loaded into the computer at the conclusion of the deal, the lenders appreciate it, the buyer gets approved much more quickly!

After finishing with all of the information, have the buyers sign the application.

Since you have not received the exact amounts given you by the manager, the offer is less than asked for. Consequently, you may not say you have a deal. Don't put your foot in your mouth by saying you *think* you have a deal.

Simply say something along the lines of, "Keep your fingers crossed while I see if my manager can make this deal work. Be just a few moments so don't get too excited . . .". Act like our old TV hero: Columbo.

You don't want them to think the deal is done and have your manager "bump" their offer . . . even if their offer is a decent one . . . since it could have the adverse affect of "twisting" your buyer and making the deal, even if made, less than happy. Remember, for this deal and later, customer service and relationships are everything!

Take the "cash", worksheet with the buyer's commitment on it, the trade-in evaluation form and the credit application to your manager. That's the guy with the wide butt sitting in the sales tower. Big grin! Rich guy! Pays alimony to two ladies with the child support as an "add-on".

Or the fairly rare lady desk manager who keeps a husband at home in art supplies to follow his destiny. She remains pragmatic in her view on life.

Both, absolutely, surely, positively want to and will make your deal.

Just has to make sense.

That's why they make the BIG bucks.

And, my aspiring and talented representative, you may grow up and be just like them!

Since right now, as you have dropped off all of the info they need to really get the ball rolling, print out the invoice of the vehicle you're dealing on; the credit bureau is being requested; the "used car buyer", or wholesaler, is given the evaluation form to really bid the trade to get a real value.

. . . . and now your manager is going to "pencil" you back with other figures since most of the input needed, after a glance at the "Blue Book", shows where you are in the deal.

Hold on to your horses . . . getting close!

Chances are, unless this is your first or second deal, you're going back in with the adjusted figures.

You wonder, since you felt the figures weren't that far off, why the "pencil" is a bit higher that expected.

Remember, when a sky diver jumps from the plane, he can always go down but can't go back up.

And you can always lower the price if it makes sense to make the deal. The opposite just doesn't do so well.

Same way in the deal. If the desk manager is worth his/her salt even a little bit, even a great offer is countered with at least a little higher offer. Human nature being what it is, people will not be as satisfied with the overall sale if they are to forever wonder if they had offered TOO much. That's just what most feel when someone takes your first offer. That they should have offered less.

Believe it or not, most folks do like to barter whether they will admit it or not. What you learn is to what degree your particular customer is willing to go in the negotiations and keep them in the "Happy Zone".

Not to be confused with actor Robin Williams idea of "Mr. Happy".

Re-entering your office or cubicle with your customer, you now have the makings of a deal. It's just a little more money than you took from them as an offer to your manager. It's looking good.

Why? Because you are excited! That is your attitude. You have worked hard for them. And you share their fortune!

All of that, plus the fact that while you were away, they pondered some of the trial closes you suggested previously. They have been doing the math of the deal. In short, they have started to mentally take possession.

Now you be cookin'!

You have in your hand a "pencil" that you present to the buyer. It shows the deal will need $2,500 cash with monthly payments from $435-$455.

Your possible presentation might be, "Great news! For only $1500 and $60 a month (more), we DO have a deal!"

Your buyer is looking at the paper as you are saying this. He sees $2,500 cash. He sees the $455 a month.

Since you already had a firm commitment from before, you only need to "bump" the little bit extra. No scam. Just practicality.

There may be yet another compromise. Chances are, there will. With the next offer, perhaps $1800 cash and $435 a month (The buyer: "I'm going to pay the smaller payment. NO WAY will I pay that extra $20 for nothing! You can do that or I'm out of the market!")

Your response might be, "Okay . . . let me try it again. You just sit here and ponder where you'll be taking your first vacation with your new car."

So, off you go. To the tower. The grin. The butt.

The deal.

Now may be the time for the next step.

Step 12: Turn the deal to Management.

Depending on the activity at the dealership, now is usually a good time for a little extra special touch for the customer. It's nice to reinforce good feelings and the sense of a good deal. Regardless of how well you may have done your job, it's nice to share it with the others involved. Not to be like Pollyanna, but it's one big happy family there at the dealership and you're bringing your new buyers into the fold.

Accordingly, a "bigger badge" is appreciated since it shows a special touch. The desk manager who has been doing the "penciling" all along is the first choice to come in to thank and greet your buyers. Occasionally, the assistant manager may do the honors. The new, and maybe last, "pencil" would be in hand.

It may be that the deal proposed by the manager is just $2,100 cash, or only $300 more from the buyer. The monthly payment may be $444 a month, just $7 more a month.

And nine times out of ten, the deal would be done with the final numbers preceded by a congratulatory approach by the manager. "I certainly want to thank you folks for allowing us to earn your business. I am the manager here: Benevolent Butts. Most call me Ben. I know that I can feel safe in knowing that $7 a month and $300 is certainly putting you into your new vehicle."

Etc., Etc.

Making his exit, a buyers order will be drawn up. You will pick up a complete package with all of the necessary forms and complete them along with your buyer. Your buyer's new vehicle will be on the way to being detailed and (perhaps) filled with fuel. There are lot attendants in most cases to take care of that. It is YOUR responsibility, though, to make certain it is done and done well.

That's what you will be doing in a bit after you have set your buyers to be scheduled to meet in the business office with a finance manager.

Okay. All of the paperwork is done on your end. You have taken the completed file to the desk manager and he/she has added additional forms belonging to the deal. The deal is signed off, you take it to the business office and sign your people in. Allow your customers to wait in the lounge while you pay attention to the figurehead of all the work that you have been doing: the new vehicle.

As I said, bigger dealerships would usually have lot attendants to take care of getting the vehicle detailed. On the other hand, you may have to get it done yourself in situations beyond your control. Don't cry. Just do it! You are working for your people and you will be asking for referrals. Now you will earn the right to do so.

So, now the car is detailed. In and out, spiffy! There are little suggestions learned through experience that are considerate and remembered by customers for a long time. Such as, you may want to set the radio to the channels that were set in the trade-in vehicle. A safe assumption could be had that the buyer likes the stations that he or she set. (Duh!) You may want to (after the buyer has cleaned out their trade) place their items in the new vehicle. Put the garage door opener on the visor. Visually inspect under the hood so there are no surprises.

During this time, your buyers have been with the finance manager going over the payments, perhaps considering disability and life (choke and croak), extended warranties, desert protection packages (mop and slop) and so on. They are fine. You have time.

So now you move to

Step 13: Record your deal.

As dealerships are becoming more organized, there are customer logs dictating the activity of the customers. Who was here with whom? When? Address? Phone? Vehicle interested in? Etceteras.

And was it a **sold** deal?

The company logs typically expand that "etceteras" portion to meaning, in addition what was stated, a collection of information that can be helpful in making a car deal.

For example, a log sheet may have boxes indicating: 'Was there a Demo given?'; 'Did management speak with the customer?'; 'The stock number of the vehicle interested in'; Did the salesperson "write up" the customer?; 'Was the customer an appointment, referral or an 'up'?; 'E-mail address'; 'Description of trade-in'; 'Manager approval box'; and an area for any pertinent comments.

This is where you would want to update everything that needed said updating. Such as, what was bought and traded on the deal when a deal was finalized.

This information is an outstanding feature to have when any following up is done. There is enough insight for others representing the dealership to understand how to approach a potential customer.

This all helps you when you're doing your job. It helps the dealership when you're not.

It helps the customer when a deal was missed!

Baby step to some but important nonetheless.

That brings us to

Step 14: Delivery.

This is probably one of the most overlooked of all of the easy things in sales. It is so easy to let your guard down now that all has gone well. You are about to cross the finish line. Don't blow it. Five deals or more down the road depend on the final yards of this sale.

It is the time to put the ribbon on the package with a sincere, efficient and thorough delivery of the buyers conquest.

Although many dealerships have dedicated delivery specialists, the personal touch by you, their salesperson, adds quite a bit. Particularly when you have grown to know them a bit and know just what is important to them.

You or the delivery coordinator will present the owners with the manufacturer's manual. You will go over the necessary pamphlets and such and leave them with understanding of how it all applies to them.

You will impress upon the buyer how important it is to you and the dealership to get not only a great report when the buyer is surveyed, but a MAGNIFICENT report! All 'A's. Perfect! Top of the class!

Because you've earned it!

And you're still earning it.

Get their assurances that excellent marks are just what they will check on the survey when the manufacturer sends the it to them. If you have earned it, and I know you have, they will do it. People do like to pay tribute when it is earned.

I can tell you that I have never, and I do mean never, given anything less than excellent when I have returned surveys. Not because all in a deal is perfect, necessarily, but I can tell you I most likely would not have done the deal at all if it was not a good, I mean excellent, one.

I felt good doing it, too.

It does make a huge difference to you and your dealership to get high marks. You will find out how and why but I can tell you it hits home right at "Hip National Bank".

So, alright, you and the delivery gal and guy have done the manuals. Now, take them through a quick check through the dealership and point out the service department, the parts department, the body shop. Show just how complete and great your team really is. You show that you appreciate their business and you want to continue to earn it in the future.

Now, they were a little distracted when you were doing your sales presentation earlier. Efficiently, since they are tired and "just want to go home", review the bells and whistles in the interior of the vehicle. Make sure they are comfortable. Help to adjust the seats for them.

Acquaint them with the fluid checks under the hood. It's their car, now, and they need to know. Show the spare and tools to replace the tire.

I think that's all. Do a little thinking on your own. I'm getting a little tired. Actually, you'll do fine. Just use your noggin. I trust you.

Anyhow, I wanted to get to

Step 15: Follow your Customer.

And not necessarily out of the dealership to their home. Unless, of course, you need to follow them home for the title of the trade or to pick up the check they didn't have on them when they purchased the vehicle.

After all, they were "just looking", remember?

What is really being referred to here is to follow them up with phone calls and letters to make sure everything related to their buying experience was all that you promised. In the event you had a customer that didn't purchase ("Be Backs"), it's obvious why one would want to follow up. "Buy or Die" is the motto of many successful sales people. That doesn't mean you're rude or crude. It means you care enough to make sure the customer gets what they really want or need.

So, you follow up. With those who buy and those who don't.

You create a tracking system to periodically make contact with anyone who may or may not be making a purchasing decision in the next week or next five years. This is not only courteous, it is professional!

Remember this, kids, that the difference between amateurism and professionalism is that one does it without getting paid and the other gets paid. You figure out which class you want to be associated with.

In a well run, organized dealership, managers make sure that the logs of customers are used to make contact. Customer service will call the buyers of the vehicles to make sure all is well and if there are any other services needed. Reminders are given to the purchasers about the free oil changes and inspections that may be offered.

For those who didn't buy yet, reminders will be given of why they should make their purchase NOW instead of waiting. Know this: if you do not follow up with your customers, someone else will! There goes a commission for that one. There goes three or more referrals.

Remember, too, that even one sale can make a huge difference in your own life. That could mean your own car payment, your rent or mortgage payment, the boat that you have been promising yourself since Moby Dick was a minnow.

The most successful of sales people have customer base records that have been sold to other sales professionals for thousands of dollars. That can't be stated too often. It's because they have a huge and obvious worth. That base has been cultivated and weeded and watered and nourished for years.

Harvesting is its own reward.

CHAPTER 7

TRIAL CLOSES

In the course of presenting a product, reading between the lines may give an indication as to how an approach may be as effective as possible. What is the mindset of the buyer? What are the "hot buttons"? Are they really 'just looking' or are they waiting to meet a salesperson? Are they playing games? Do they think *I'm* playing games?

Of course, it still gets down to a very simple concept: **communication**.

We have been there: done that. What I am offering here are what are known as 'Trial Closes' and can help both the buyer and seller make a mutually satisfying car deal.

Trial closes are just what they appear to be: a way of testing the water and seeing if it's safe to jump in: or not.

They aren't meant to overcome objections so much as they are to indicate true feelings, plant seeds of thought and indicate directions in which to go.

This is yet another tool in a salesperson's handbag that's designed to do a thorough and qualified job of satisfying what we've come to realize 'Sales' is all about: mutual satisfaction. Notice that I come back to that since buying and selling is in the same package. Mirror image. Yin and Yang. Without the one, the other is non-existent.

So, how do you make the best deal? (Who was I referring to? The buyer or the seller?)

Yes, Hopalong, you got it . . . to the both of you. Or the same one. Since we are all one or the other at any given moment.

So, if you're the buyer, give yourself these trial closes. Do they work? Make sense? Help you sort your thoughts?

Of course, as the seller, you can be expected to know these since it's your job to do just that. A buyer isn't always as fortunate. Unless they have had the pleasure of meeting you to help them along in what they may want or need anyhow.

You have to take to heart that you're here on Earth to help others. But, if that's true, what are the others on Earth for?

A thought to ponder.

Before you get too brain locked, here are some examples of trial closes. For those of you in the audience, please feel free to join in! There are more. Lots more. These are just some examples that are tried and true. (That's where the pseudo-intellectual would have said, ". . . if you will").

Stupid me.

So I won't say it.

When you have earned the right, established rapport, gotten a feel for the buyer's wants and needs, inject these comments and questions accordingly.

For instance, on the test drive, the buyer is a little more relaxed and consequently is receptive to not only questions but of your opinions. Again, keep the buyer's objective in mind.

I have stated that a final close can be used at any time, as well as now, but assuming this is not the time, your goal is to keep the buyer thinking in the "Yes" mode. Repeat: Saying and thinking 'Yes' sets the brain up to continue the positive process.

This may, or may not work on first dates. The same may be true with customers. We won't go into trial closes for first dates. We'll leave that for the next edition by one of the many given sports heroes of the moment to publish.

We also won't delve into 'trial closes' for trials used by the attorney representing the given sports hero.

Here are some examples for the automobile transaction:

1) "How will this vehicle look in your driveway?"
2) "Will it fit well in your garage?"
3) "Who will be the most envious—your neighbor, maybe?"
4) "Will you be taking this on your next vacation?"

5) "Who will you show it to first?"
6) "I guess you'll get some jealous ribbing from your co-workers, huh?"
7) "I would guess this vehicle could open up new avenues for you with your profession!"
8) "Will you miss leaving the spare parts and tools from your other vehicle behind?"
9) "This vehicle seems to be equipped the way you suggested!"
10) "Do you think your old vehicle will miss you?"
11) "How will you be taking title to your new car? Will it be in your name alone or with your (wife/husband)?"
12) "What do like the most about this vehicle?"
13) "We actually only keep 25% to 30% of the vehicles we take in on trade. We need yours!"
14) "We have immediate delivery with on site financing!"
15) "Will you allow your (wife/husband) to drive the new vehicle?"
16) "Jimmy Buffet (or Andy Williams, Boston Symphony, Roseanne, or Snoopy Pup Canine Doggy) will sure put you in Heaven with this sound system!"(If your customer is alone, be ready for "snide" remark!)
17) "Who will be driving the new car home?"
18) "You deserve this car!"
19) "Just pull the car in the 'Sold' line."
20) "Just sign the 'Sold' ticket."
21) "If all of the details can be worked out, is this the vehicle you will buy today? I mean, right now?"

Surely, there are a great deal more trial closes you could think of. The point is to get to the point of *asking for the sale!*

These help to get you there! Again, way too many otherwise qualified sales people could be so much better if they would just ASK FOR THE SALE!

For those of you who may have forgotten about the point of selling cars and have been dwelling on "lines" to ask for dates, some of the trial closes can use appropriate substitutions for 'vehicles' or 'cars' and be applied in said fashion. Example: "You deserve this body."

Good luck.

Before moving onto some examples of 'Closes' used to overcome objections and, I would guess, *close* a deal, I just wanted to point out some examples of "fact finding" questions used early in the relationship. I try not to put the cart before the horse but I wanted to show some examples as not to confuse them with trial closes.

Fact finding does just what?

Rebecca, in the front row: you're waving your hand! Wildly!

Yes, dear, that's right! You DO find facts.

Information: Leads to good communication; Same language, Same song sheet and Insight.

Here are some examples to reiterate what types of questions would be fact finding in nature:

1) "What brought you to the dealership?"
2) "What type of work do you do? Been doing it long? Which company?"
3) "How large is your family?"
4) "Have you been to "Belchfire Motors" before?"
5) "Do you live in the area? Oh, really! I used to live near there: in the Springwood Apt. complex. Do you live near there or do you own your home? How long?"
6) "Will there be anyone else in helping to make your buying decision?"
7) "Who will be the primary driver?"
8) "What do you like about your present car? What don't you like?"
9) "How long have you had you current vehicle? Is it the only vehicle in the family? Second? Third?"
10) "Did you buy it new or used?"
11) "Do you have an extended warranty on your vehicle?"
12) "Have you done anything to the vehicle to enhance the value? Upgrade the stereo, for instance?"
13) "Have you owned a (dealership's line of vehicles) "Belchfire" before?"
14) "How do you plan on using the vehicle?"

15) "Would this be the primary vehicle? For the family?"
16) "What would you like to have in your new vehicle that you don't currently have?"
17) "How many miles do you drive?"(month or year)
18) "Any idea where preparations 'A' through 'G' went to?"

Alright. I guess number 18 shouldn't come up in fact finding. I guess you see the point, though. I might mention that it may appear there are contradictions with regards to steps in meeting the customer. There are times, you know, that a person is expected to think in a standing position. On your feet.

The more you know about where you are trying to travel to, the easier the trip will be. Be aware of when, what and where in the relationship these things are brought up.

Just think!

The saga of Org and Tumba gave some exaggerated and outrageous examples of closes. In the real world, the closes serve to close because they are based on fact, common sense, and perceptual suggestions. The perception that something costs too much may be countered by asking, "Compared to what?"

The suggestion by a customer that the other dealer could give a better deal has to be countered by, "Are we comparing apples to apples? Is it the same model? Trim level? Is the vehicle in stock?"

Even if the answers are yes, yes, yes and again, yes . . . why, oh why are they with you here and now?

I can tell you. Yea, I know . . . you've already guessed. The customer has yet to meet a salesman or saleswoman or salesperson. And the customer doesn't know how to sell his money, either. Sometimes, there are no sales people in the deal whatsoever!

The search is still on for the deal that is mutually satisfying. "Org-asmic" and "Tumba-esque". Evolutionary.

The person in search for a vehicle has yet to find a dealership to sell his money to. He really is trying, you know. The dealer just hasn't learned how to buy his money. So, here you are. A very good buyer. You know how to buy the money the customer has to offer with some old steel, plastic and rubber.

It's all the same. Mirror image. If the customer doesn't know yet, get over the edge. Impress upon the customer the need to sell: from his perspective.

You need to buy the customer's money, after all.

Offer enough value in the rubber and steel so you CAN buy it.

CHAPTER 8

OVERCOMING OBJECTIONS

(Just another way of saying "Closes")

A variety of scenarios can occur when you're sitting with the customer where, for whatever reason, someone apparently wanting a car can come up with a plethora of reasons for NOT wanting one.

There are a number of types of objections. There are different personalities that supply them. Overall, there are only two types of objections, though. One is *real*. The other is a *stated* objection.

I have come to experience various sub-varieties of "objectors. I am certain there remain a sub-sub-variety but life is too short to go there.

Imagine after you have spent a fair amount of time with the customer. You are together in your office or cubicle working out all of the details to your transaction. Numbers and choices are presented to consummate this deal and you feel, hear or see the objections coming.

One may be in the form of the "information gatherer". He's the one wanting to know technical facts or comparisons to other vehicles that may be in competition to your product.

Another is the "cynical" buyer. You feel as if everything you may offer or toss out there has to be an absolute and proven fact. Nothing seems to be good enough! If you state that the car gets 33 miles per gallon in fuel use, it had better be so.

Yet another: the "stated" buyer. This individual goes back to the premise that "he was just looking, anyway; Wasn't planning on doing a deal; Don't even have my checkbook. Etc., etc." This objector blows smoke because, well, because he can. This buyer claims he's "Just not sure, yet".

Then, we have the "Rooster". The rooster knows it all! The rooster either has known someone "well" who did your job for years or did it himself (for 2 months or so) and knows all that there is to know about this line of work. The rooster tends to have an ego that needs adjusted.

Now and then, we all come across someone who is just plain *mean*. I mean, they just get off on making people around them feel uncomfortable by badgering and belittling them. This type of person may attack you (verbally only, or the "federales" may have to be called in), your dealership, the city you're in and the entire industry of automobile manufacturing. Nasty motor scooter, he is.

The *teetering* objector is one who is just unsure of himself. Questions such as, "How do I know this is the best deal out there on this car?"; "I wonder if maybe I shouldn't get a two door instead?"; "Oh, my . . . I just am so *worried* I may just lose my job and then what would I do?".

Well, you get the idea. There are a lot of varieties of us out there in this world. Makes it interesting. What isn't so interesting is when this gets in your way of making the deal. So, let's put some more tools in your briefcase and deal with them as a plumber would with a leak.

That's by using the right tools and materials for the right situation.

You know, I have been around some of the most experienced, practical and proficient closers in the auto industry. Absolutely terrific mentors! They're among those at the top 'o' the heap; the thrill of making the deal was always present and had a life of its own. You could *feel* it! To go for the close and get to the top of the box you have been building is such a wonderful and fulfilling feeling. Everyone is happy: You; Them; Everyone!

Just what does it take to close a deal? Experience? Instinct? Knowledge? Your product? Psychology? Logic?

To name a few: yessir and ma'am.

I've said the 'close' is always present. I have experienced that precise moment within the first few moments of a deal. Instinctively.

Perhaps to an outsider, the word 'close' sounds very cold and impersonal. Perhaps . . . but without maybe realizing it, the application of it is common in our everyday lives.

I have stated and you have heard that there are basic drives that exist in all of humanity. Waxing philosophically I won't do. I will address the areas of 'food', 'shelter', and procreation. Of course, that would involve companionship and the love of others.

I heard Jerry Seinfeld say that *all* men know what they want: *WOMEN*!

The problem lies in understanding and how to get them!

Take an example: A man spies a woman at a quaint cafe. Surroundings smother one in a continental flavor: rich, full aromas thick of international blends of coffees accented by the rich, dark chocolates poured not an hour before. Freshly baked croissants place the touching memory of a time long past in your grandmother's kitchen. Bonnie Raitt sings a bluesy rendition to strum the bass of your soul.

All of this ambience strikes out to a deep, emotional need to fill the abyss the man had not realized even existed until he had caught the way the woman had flipped her hair back. This action accented the perfectly unique manner in which she puckered her perfectly formed and highlighted lips.

Gathering courage, he casually strolls over . . . runs his fingers through his hair . . . wipes at the corners of his mouth.

Looping his thumbs in his pockets, he notices an almost imperceptible shift to her eyes; followed by a hint of a smile.

Mating game, he thinks.

Heart building rate, adrenaline joining suit, he smoothly and ever so lightly places a hand upon her shoulder.

She turns, a questioning smile fixed in her stare, and says, "Yes?"

He freezes! He knows what he wants! He knows just how good of a guy he is. *The moment of truth,* he thinks to himself.

Mouth starts to perform a function. He speaks.

"Wanna bump?" (Other more crude terms could have been used but my writing is PG13 at worst.)

Well, she didn't.

No sale. No steps. No good.

No close! One wasn't needed because there weren't any that would work. At least with this guy. Backing up, he could use a few steps, but his "commission" would *definitely* be a mini!

Again, making a point. Have fun with this. Use it every day. But then, you have, haven't you?

Having gotten this far, you have done well. The closes, coming up, are yours to use.

As you will realize, some of these closes are such that they could be used not only in car sales but in life and other types of sales, as well. One more plug for coffee houses here.

As it has been said, nothing sells like the truth. That is just what a close is: bringing the truth to surface and applying it to the situation in hand.

Let's list a few, shall we?

List of Closes

1) Ben Franklin Close.

This is a close that would be used when the buyer is perhaps a little "wishy-washy" about the deal. They may be worried about the cost, down payment, practicality of buying, or perhaps a little guilt has entered the soul and there are feelings of not deserving it. Whatever. This close ties down the deal.

This close is also known as a 'Pro/Con' close. Since the days of 'Poor Richard' writing his Almanac, many a situation has been called upon to compare what is *good* about the deal and what is *poor* about the deal. In a given car deal, there will probably be some items that are on the 'poor', or not so good, or 'con' side. They should be acknowledged as well as the 'good', or 'pro' side.

This close depends on the shared knowledge of what the benefits may, or may not, be. It certainly depends on the ability of the salesperson to overwhelm the 'cons' with 'pros' since there otherwise wouldn't be much sense in doing the deal.

Understand there are any number of items that can be used: financial, practical, emotional, frivolous, or material means.

A chart should be shared with open dialogue and writing down the items as they come to mind by both the buyer and seller.

By the very virtue that the buyer is sitting across from you, the positive side will certainly overpower the negative side.

Continue on to see an example of presenting this form of close:

PRO'S	CON'S
New Car	BIG repair bill coming
Better gas mileage	$2+/gal. for gas: gas hog!
Warranty	Huge, unknown cost to repair current
No repair bill	More costly!
New safety features protects family	Old features match bald tires!
Save: payment less than old payment plus	Current pmt. on "lesser" vehicle
repairs	New payment
More room	Already used to ripped seat and
Better ride and comfort (no back pain, maybe?)	spring in butt!
You deserve it! (What do you work for, anyhow?)	I like adding a quart of oil every day!
No more aggravation!	
Shows mother-in-law how you're a success!	
Your friends will envy you!	
It's not your OLD car!	
. . . and so on	

As you can see, there are an unlimited number of ways and items that could be suggested. Use your personality and lighten it up if it's called for. Be pragmatic if necessary. It is merely a way to come to a decision where one school of thought outweighs another.

Again I state that the buyer is there and wants it. Help the deal out by giving all of the reasons to do what is right!

2) Gas Mileage Close.

This is another close that uses simple, mathematical knowledge with a savings approach. Already, there are reasons to see that closes may come in groups. And we would only have a "group" of two at this point.

The gas savings on a new vehicle would certainly make a positive point in the Ben Franklin approach.

This is going just a bit farther in showing how what may have been perceived as more costly may, in fact, show savings in the greater whole.

Using the fact that the customer has a fairly regular schedule of driving 2,000 miles in a month for both work and pleasure, let's see how we can make some sense out of this.

We have the buyer's current vehicle getting 12 m.p.g. of gasoline.

Your new vehicle shows an average consumption of 28 m.p.g. of gasoline.

We will use the cost of gas at $2.25 per gallon even though as I write this the cost exceeds $3.00 a gallon in some areas of the country.

The customer is concerned about the monthly payment you have presented. Where $350 a month payment would be comfortable to him, the payment of $430 seems more than could be afforded. Illustrate as shown:

Current Vehicle	
Miles driven a month:	2,000
(divided by)M.P.G.	12
Number of gallons/mo.=	167
(Rounded from 166.67)	
At $2.25/gal., monthly cost =	$375
New Vehicle	
Same miles per month	2,000
(divided by)M.P.G.	28
Number of gallons/mo. =	71
(Rounded from 71.43)	
At same $2.25/gal.,	
Monthly cost =	$160

Difference in savings to the customer with the new vehicle would be $215 in one month!

Considering the monthly payments of $350 (wants) and $430 (too high!) are $80 apart, it is easily shown that in fact, based on the buyer's own numbers, the savings of $215 less the $80 difference in payment still leaves $135 to benefit the buyer!

A case could further be made that with that $135 in savings added to the $430, the break even point would be $565 a month! One could show the point that the customer is losing money as he's staring you in the eye!

W HOOOOOOOOOWHEEEEEEEEEEEE!!!!!

We don't even *need* $565 a month, Mr. Buyer! $430 is all!

On a side note, since the buyer said he usually bought a car every five years, it could be pointed out that over a five year period there would be nearly $13,000 in fuel savings!

And to think there was a problem trying to get a cash down payment! Shame on you with such a good deal!

I just don't know how we do it and stay in business!

Oh, and one more thing for some of you out there: with the popularity of S.U.V.'s these days, and considering a Honda Civic could be the trade, this close may not be the one you would be looking for.

Thought I would mention it.

3) Reconditioning (or Re-Con) Close.

Consider a customer who is balking over (gosh, who woulda guessed?) the overall cost or down payment on a new car. The customer says that his current vehicle is fine, thank you very much, and it's good for another 50,000 miles.

"But", you ask, "at what cost?"

Along with other potential expenses associated with a "very experienced" vehicle, there are most probably costs that have to be confronted at the here and now.

In your own evaluation of the trade, you pointed out the four tires that needed replacing, the brakes that were giving a 'steel to steel' squeal, the registration plates were about to expire and emissions were required, the windshield had a crack in it making it less than safe for not only the driver but other passengers, as well.

The air conditioning was alright if you were in Fairbanks, Alaska, but otherwise this was another repair that needed to be addressed.

Even if the customer wasn't concerned with the fading paint and dented bumpers, the evidence of leaking constant velocity joints on the front wheel drive car would need more than a casual glance unless someone wanted to be stranded by the side of the road.

Cost to keep driving current vehicle:

Four tires @ $100/each:	$400
Brake job:	$350
Windshield (insurance covers, but still a pain to do)	$N/C
Air conditioning (????)	$1200
Drive joints	$350
Total	$2300

Now, if the customer was balking at dipping in to "Hip National" for a down payment, have him consider that costs will be incurred whether it's for a new car or a new one. Furthermore, if $2300 was put out for repairs the vehicle would only be brought up to average in trade in value. Essentially, the money would be "invested" in an extremely used item; money that ultimately needs to be spent one way or another.

Wouldn't it make a whole lot more sense to invest the same money in a new vehicle than in a used one? One that is already at the top of its game? One that has a full warranty included?

Remember to point out that these are only the items needed repair that you, as a sales rep, not a mechanic, noticed. Imagine what might be wrong that has passed unnoticed and what may go wrong in the near future.

Ahhhhhh, to spend all of that money that you say you don't have . . . and to only have to do it unannounced perhaps in the near future.

It only makes economic and common sense to put your money in a more secure investment, Mr. Customer.

The new vehicle you have chosen will be a total relief to you. The paint and bumpers are really pretty, too!

4) Reduce to Ridiculous Close.

Typically, this is a close used to make up the difference in payment needed from where the customer is already committed. Psychologically, as you are well aware, we all have our comfort areas and payments. For years, perhaps a person liked the $150 payment for a car. As costs increased through the years, a $250 was adjusted to. It's just a matter of math. Then, $325 a month was fine. It was in the budget and it was alright. Costs were increasing and still are. It is still a mental adjustment started with a dose of reality a while back and continues to adjust periodically. Of course, off-setting increases in the average salary helps with the justification of the adjustments.

Well, reality is still happening. Some of us may not like it, but there it is! It is fortunate that a customer has you right there to show this in a light that is in a totally acceptable manner. It is so pain free. And an honest to goodness truth.

So, you have your customer very used to the $325 a month payment. Knowing that costs are more and a minimum cash down payment would be preferred, the customer may well be okay with a little more payment. Like maybe $350. But absolutely, positively, monkey be nailed to a cross . . . no more than that.

Needing the payment to be $385 a month, you are $35 away from making a deal.

For this observation, I did make a simple example. I know it. You will, too.

It is only $35. The customer is already $25 over where the ideal payment would be. But that is ignored by you since it's already given. I mention it only to give you a feeling of the buyer's psyche. Neat word, that. Psyche.

So, let's use it again. Psyche. Let's 'psych' the buyer up! Show just how easy this is. You have a deal.

You are talking about roughly a dollar a day. That's all! It's a soda pop: just like the one you had already bought the customer.

Maybe the customer needs another. It's insignificant as a cost, after all.

And that REALLY is the only thing keeping the customer from taking home this car of choice: a soda pop! Gosh, who couldn't give up just one soda a day? Or two cigarettes? Or a pack of cigarettes (wow! That would be like $250 to $400 a month for two pack a day smokers). Be careful with the smokers, though. No one really likes to be preached to about morals. A couple of cigarettes mentioned makes the point, though.

It could be mentioned that people stop at 'Moonbucks' for coffee in the morning. How about taking your own coffee from home? That could be $60 a month in money saved.

Or what about the paper bought every day when there is one to be read at work. That could be another $15 a month.

Lunch at $5 per day minimum: nobody spends less than that! But that amounts equals $150 per month compared to probably only $50 per month spent if the person 'brown bagged' it.

Would *you* not give up a soda or bottled water a day to have a new car? Wouldn't you eat better by taking your lunch to work and saving $100 to boot?

Just two cigarettes out of forty smoked a day could be the deal maker. Would you skip those two cigarettes to have this new car?

Of course!

Who would not? It costs less than you may think. And not very ridiculous, at that!

5) Forced Savings Close.

This is a close that could be used to either gather more of a down payment or more in the way of payment. It could also make the payment that is really preferred more attractive. It suggests to anyone that plans on ever buying a car again or one who ever plans on paying off the car and *never* buying another car (thinking: who did I leave out?) that it is perhaps in the buyer's best interest to pay more for the vehicle in lump sums or by paying more monthly. It only stands to reason that the more that is paid towards the vehicle would make less owed on the vehicle in the future. If a person put down $2,000 on a $20,000 purchase, $18,000 would be the amount financed.

At 8% interest over five years, the payment would be $364.98.

If $4,000, rather than $2,000, were put down, the amount financed would be $16,000 and with the same terms the payment would be $324.42.

With one fell stroke, $2,000 of future inequity is thus avoided. Regardless of it were to happen in a year or three years, there would be $2,000 less to consider for a payoff in a trade or outright sale.

If the additional down payment just could not happen, it could be shown that perhaps the buyer would be in a better condition down the pike if the payment was adjusted only slightly upwards to $400. The same loan of $18,000 could be paid in full in only four and one half years! That would save six months of interest and regardless of when the possible trade or sale of the vehicle could occur, there would be more equity.

It's like a 'Christmas Club' for your car!

When I have had the occasion to use this close, more often than not it would be to shoot higher on down payment or monthly payment to show the payment needed to make the deal as just that much more reasonable. Most people like the idea of paying off earlier but the reality factor comes in and they end up liking the lower payments.

That is why the producer in F&I makes a good case to take the loan term to 72 or more months. That $364.98 payment would be $315.60 using the same 8% rate at six years, or 72 months. It's easy to show the benefits of that. It looks a lot easier to handle and could be shown that the borrower could always pay more towards the principal to pay the loan off in a shorter time. That's what we were talking about, anyway.

It is shown that a large amount of consumers are extremely optimistic about paying off early. That is why furniture stores, mattress outlets, building supply centers and the like often offer 0% for three months to a year of deferred interest since people plan to pay it off before that time arises.

Enough consumers don't pay off the balance to avoid the 20% to 24% common rates with those programs so it remains lucrative for the extenders of these programs. New sales are created and new income is derived from the extended terms.

Human nature deserves to be further observed: for better . . . for worse.

6) Isolating Objections and Tie Downs

Frequently, customers resort to the language of "boogey". We've been there, done that. I know this. I just want to show that, in a sense, being able to isolate what the *real* objection is and then coming to a remedy is a close unto itself. It's pretty apparent, huh? Hearing a statement such as, "That's too much!" might warrant a response such as, "Compared to what?"

Or, "I am not planning on buying today." You could address with, "Why not?"

Take this one: "Even though I am not doing the deal today, I will come to see you when I am ready to buy."

You could respond with, "Thank you very much. I have enjoyed you, as well. Let me ask, though, if I could save you the return trip along with a great deal of savings, wouldn't it make sense to do the deal now?"

"No."

"Why?", you ask.

Chances are, by eliminating all of the 'no's' in the objections, you will come on to the 'yes' in the equation. That is why the word 'no' can be a truly beautiful word. You can always depend upon the 'yes' laying five degrees to the right and due north of it.

There is ALWAYS a reason to buy now. If the unit is available: Or, if it isn't; If the customer has a checkbook or if it was forgotten; If the sun is out or there is an eclipse.

Isolate the objection. Concentrate on making the remedy necessary to that objection so it no longer is viable. Switch shoes. What would it take in your position if your were wearing your customer's shoes? Would you not appreciate someone looking so hard to help you save and get what is wanted?

Yes, you would. I would, too.

The customer may say, "That's too much money!"

You may ask, "Compared to what?"

The customer may be easy. He may say, "The payment is too high."

If that is the only objection to making a deal, it's easily answered by asking, "If we can get the payment to your satisfaction, would you take the deal right here and right now?"

The customer will either say yes, no or maybe. Keep isolating and address the barrier. If it was only the payment, work on the numbers to make it work.

If the answer is 'no', you would, of course, ask "Why not?"

There may be another objection that you can address with the previous objection.

Statements such as, "If we could do the 'x', 'y' and the 'z', you would do that . . . wouldn't you?"

If the reply is 'yes' or 'maybe', get to work. If it is 'no', get to work and isolate the objection some more.

The words 'why', 'why not', 'wouldn't you', all invite a response. Tie downs used at the end of a statement or question are meant to do just that: tie down a commitment or narrow the search in rooting out the *true* objection.

Get used to trying it at work and play. You'll find how easy it is to get and give a little.

You'll do that. Won't you?

The word 'no' can actually start looking to be a little bit of an attraction.

Who knew?

7) Feel, Felt, Found.

Having been used for mucho many moons, this approach is one in which the salesperson wants to extend some compassion, empathy and promote a common bond. There are times in all of our dealing where things happen that are less than enjoyable. There are experiences that people don't wish to share or to repeat again.

Objections, accusations, false bravado and even just plain old nervousness can be handled with a little bit of patience with a little bit of sharing.

For instance, a customer may not realize all of the new technology that has been developed since 1962, the last year of purchasing a vehicle this person has experienced. Having gotten used to a pickup truck, the carrying ability was still wanted but the customer wasn't sure if she could put up with less than a smooth ride.

(I know this sounds off the wall in these times. There are so many commercials and such that you would think that every person is up on things. This is, however, based on a real deal. The lady had a truck approaching 40 years old and never watched television and seldom listened to any commercials on the radio. She thought she needed a better ride for her "rheumatism" but liked to have her "things' in the back of the truck.)

Approaching her remark with, "I can see just how you *feel*. You're mixed with that smooth, limo ride but you may not want to put your "things" in the back seat of a car. You know, I *felt* that way back in the '60's. For the most part, it was true. The pickups just did not have the ride the cars do. But, let me tell you, I have *found* with the new designs and suspension, the new pickups ride as well as some of your nicer cars. Other people swear they have *found* them to ride even better!"

Use this approach when it feels right. Again, you are projecting sincerity. Even if you are dealing with a customer who works in sales and remarks on what you are doing with having recognized your close, the truth in between the words will overcome any and all feelings of trickery and make the deal!

8) Split the Difference Close.

Pretty obvious already, isn't it? This is a phrase with which we have all grown to be comfortable with. To use it in a closing situation is an easily accomplished task. "Split the difference! What? Oh, bloody 'ell! Do the deal! I have 'alfway dropped me knickers to save the likes of yourself more than a quid, I'll tell you!"

That is the kicker to this. Do not be too quick to come to this conclusion. This close may be used after a fair amount of negotiating has been accomplished. Naturally, the difference price has to fall in an area where the price still reflects a favorable deal. By favorable, I always consider the best deal where all parties are satisfied. By the very nature of this book I tend to lend an eye more to the seller, of course. For those of you reading this who may be looking for a better way to purchase a vehicle or anything else, well, more power to you!

A method I have had some success with in using this close is to not go to the exact middle. For instance, if the bartering was on the difference of a payment, weigh the difference in your favor.

A payment wanted by the buyer of $350 versus the dealership's asking payment of $426 would split in the middle to $388.

After offering to split the difference, I may offer $399 per month. I know the psychological advantage of keeping the payment under $400 may outweigh the contest of "dueling to a draw".

At the very least, a buyer with more than a third grade education will point out that is not truly the split that was expected. "The difference would take the payment to $388!", cries the buyer.

Your response is a sincere one. "We need $426 a month to make this deal. I am not sure I can do it for any less. I just don't know! Know this, though: I am working to make a deal for you. For you! If we can, in fact, make this work, I know you would not let a measly eleven dollars a month, which amounts to only a quarter a day, keep you from doing the deal. One quarter! (Worked in 'Reduce to Ridiculous' close!)

"Besides, have you ever split a piece of firewood? You have? Have you ever seen one split absolutely in the middle? No?

"Neither have I! Let's give this a try. Give me your 'okay' on this offer!"

I do want to emphasize the fact that I have seen too many go to this close a little too quickly: particularly impatient closers. As a salesperson, there is an awful lot of effort put into making a deal. To so quickly put aside any potential gross profit is negligence on the part of the closer. If you are the closer, your pocket will be a little lighter at the end of the month, as well.

Make the deal with an eye towards being a mite discerning with the close being used at the proper time.

I couldn't wait any longer to move to the next close so I will leave the rest of this oh so difficult close for you to think about.

9) Use Your God Given Talent Close.

This is the ultimate deal maker! Not all of you will qualify for this, however. For those of you who do, you know who you are!

If, by some chance, you don't know, ask yourself the following questions:

1) Do you have to tie a piece of meat to your body to attract a date?
2) If you ask 'who is the fairest of them all' to the mirror, does the mirror respond, "Give me a break!" and it does?
3) When you are driving the highway, do small children in passing cars get their parents to slow down so they can get a second look at you?
4) Do they cry when they do?
5) When your mother gave birth, did the doctor slap the wrong end?
6) On a dinner date (fresh meat attached, of course), does your date order your meal for you?
7) Is it pea soup?
8) Have you ever been cited for indecent exposure when manually signaling for a turn from your car window?

If two or more of those questions are answered affirmatively, consider yourself blessed! You just may have the Gift! Not necessarily the gift of gab. Not needed!

You are, by no standards related to 'politically correct', UGLY!

Nasty, disgustingly offensive, even gruesome features CAN be used to your advantage! No steroids needed! No special health foods! No contraptions that go for a limited time offer for only $19.95. (Bur wait! There's more! If you order now, . . .)

As an employer, the dealership is well advised to immediately promote this person to 'closer' status. It is merely asking too much for a customer to spend more than a minimum of time with this person. Apparently, it truly is a talent that may overlook most of the text prior to this point. It's not needed nor is it possible to follow in your condition.

So, it is highly advised for the powers that be make you an assistant manager: a.k.a. 'Closer'.

As a Closer, your approach to the deal (walking backwards if feasible) is usually to take one of two methods in use. The first, and easiest, is to have the buyer 'okay' the deal as it is with the assurances that you will be leaving immediately, never to return!

The second way is to threaten the buyers with telling their children bedtime stories. If they have no children, threaten to tell stories to their pets.

The third way, which I didn't let you in on until now so you wouldn't *assume* anything, is to threaten to go to the buyers' neighborhood and suggest to their Home Owners Association that you are a relative and plan on moving in for the sole purpose of procreating!

Unless they do the deal!

Cruel? Yes. Effective? Absolutely!

My personal caveat is to let you know I NEVER condone this type of close, however.

I am not a sadist!

I am not a sadist!

10) Gap Close

Distance is covered in this topic. I refer to how far the future deal *could* be away from the deal being set on the table right now. The gist of this idea is merely that with historical reference, prices of goods purchased tend to go up, not down.

Since the automobile also has its own history, one of a depreciating asset, most can be assured of the value of their current vehicle will be going down in value. Additionally, with a decrease in value comes an increase in maintenance.

What the two diametrically opposed values expose (heretofore known as D.O.V.E.) is how the customer's purchasing power will take a nosedive with every passing month; perhaps every day. Looking back, the power to buy "nose-dove". (Get it?) Value guides for used car values dictate and illustrate just this with periodical publishing.

New car prices are shown increasing at a regular pace. Even with an accepted inflation indicator, the buying power of the dollar is not as strong tomorrow as it is today.

In the event a customer is indicating reluctance to buy, this could be a simple and effective way of demonstrating just these facts.

With just the statements from above, you could suggest these questions and statements while illustrating on your work sheet the diagram below.

"The trade-in value of your vehicle is going down even as we speak. Wouldn't you agree?"

"More maintenance and upkeep will be required during your ownership. Agreed? At what cost?"

"You are interested in a vehicle that is being made no more. This is the end of the year. It is unique! You *will not* see the price of this vehicle as low as this again! Ever!"

"This vehicle has had a tremendous selling record. The prices will only rise from here on out!"

"Based on the logic and common sense, and I know you are logical, it only makes sense to buy now at the best value you will ever have rather than wait and get significantly less value for your money. You work awfully hard for your money. Don't you?"

"Etc." As you are speaking, emphasize your point with this diagram:

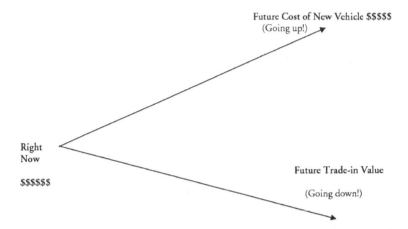

The costs are going up on what the customer wants to acquire.

The costs are going down on what the customer wishes to exchange. That is, the trade and the money it takes to do the deal.

Taken together with the 'Re-Con' close, for instance, it just makes no sense at all for a buyer to wait when the best time will never be better than the present.

Yes, the more literate of you out there will think of *'He who hesitates is lost . . . .'.*

Forsooth!

11) Three Reasons Close.

This is an approach using the concept of *isolating* the objection. I used it as a separate close since it is simple and direct in concept.

The reader should now excuse the similarity of this close to previously stated examples.

I insist!

Should you and the customer still be a ways from a deal; there may be an indication of the customer giving up. Don't *you* give up! Be understanding but find out why.

In truth, tell the customer that there are only *three* reasons a customer doesn't buy:

1) Either the customer doesn't believe what you have presented or
2) The customer doesn't understand what you have shown or
3) The customer, quite frankly, can't afford the deal!

Doesn't believe, can't understand or can't afford it!

Granted, this can be somewhat of a "standing the customer up" kind of close, but there are times when just this approach is needed. You have to decide on the way it needs to be served up. It can and should be presented in a friendly and polite manner with your focus always towards making the deal. The perception of the customer is what you will be guiding in this case. You *will* get a response and you will be in a position to isolate what the objection really happens to be.

Do you believe me?

Do you understand?

Can you afford to take the time to move on?

Right-o, then . . . .

12) Teeter Totter Close.

This close is applied when outlining the relationship of down payment versus monthly payment, for example. There are other circumstances where it could be applied but this is the first and most important reason to utilize this method of showing the give and take of more in front, less behind. Less in front, more behind (no, not a reference to the 'Desk Manager Dude' again).

It stands to reason that the more one finances, the more the payment will be. There are ways to affect the payment through the term of the loan, of course, but I am not getting into finance training here. The finance managers already know all about that.

This is the way to get more cash down to make the deal smoother, as well. Make no mistake: the more cash and equity the customer commits to the transaction, the more likely that the salesperson will stand to make more gross profit and there will be quicker acceptance by the lender financing the vehicle.

Money does talk!

There are bound to be some of you more 'quicker' witted people reading this that will draw a comparison to 'feel/felt' with 'see/saw' and I commend you for it! It could just be the mental trick needed for you to remember two whole closes!

Your mother's heart is bursting with pride, I'm sure!

Do not write feel, felt or found on this illustration as you're presenting it to the customer, though.

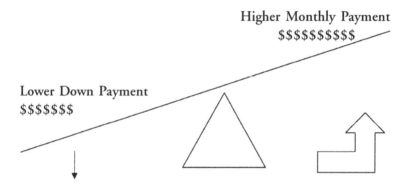

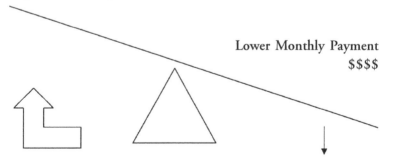

This concept and demonstration is a very easy one. The customer relates to it well and is easily presented. It works, as well.

Another case of sketching as you speak, take your real case numbers presented by the desk manager and work from there. For instance, if the deal was asking for $3,000 cash down payment and $425 a month, you would suggest to the customer that is where the deal would work.

However, the customer wants to only put $1,000 into the deal. That would leave another $2,000 to be financed.

Using $30 for every $1,000 financed, the payment would increase to $485 per month and the customer may well be okay with that. If that is the best that can be done, take the offer to the desk and see if that will do the trick.

On the flip side, by showing more of a down payment, say $5,000, you could show how to reduce the payment accordingly.

Since I am pitching and not catching, I will use $20 a month for this example. So, since the customer is placing another $2,000 into the pot over what the 'desk' had required, I would show that the payment could now be reduced to only $385 per month or thereabouts.

By demonstrating the give and take aspect with this approach, nothing at all is given up in the way of total dollar amounts. It may help the customer in adjusting how it would work the best for their own needs, though.

Hopefully, the final 'teeter' and the 'totter' will be a balanced one such as this. This is what you and the customer are both shooting for, after all.

Balanced Down Payment $$ **Balanced Monthly Payment $$**

So often the customer tends to want to put less down then what is asked for or required. This is one of the best ways to justify the cash required and make a deal that will fly through financing. At the very least, it will give some "credit challenged" folks a fighting chance to secure a loan.

This is what the desk manager had in mind all along! A deal we could all hang our hat on!

13) Take Away Close.

"The Lord doth giveth; The Lord taketh away."
Something like that: yea.

Human nature being what it is, we tend to want what we cannot possess. Around which movie star or starlet does your fantasy revolve? How magnificent is your dream mansion?

When you were a child, that Tinker Toy or Zap Phaser gun could sit undisturbed and ignored in the corner of the bedroom for eons. As soon as your brother or sister got a hold of it and was having a grand old time building or zapping, you just HAD to have it! Couldn't stand someone else playing with YOUR toy! The fight of the millennium ensued.

Something was taken away.

Every close used is an application of psychology and this is yet one more example. Nothing to do with anything other than when a person has been allowed to feel ownership and possession said person doesn't want to lose it. It's somewhat a form of losing. You've been there. It is disappointing. When you lose something, you want it back.

There can be a time when you feel you have a deal on a vehicle with the customer but it is just not done. Perhaps the customer is trying to appear elusive. Trying to get a better deal, yet. Putting on the air of non-concern and a real 'take it or leave it' attitude.

Here comes the blindside from you: fine. It certainly has been a pleasure, kind gentleperson. Here are your keys to your trade. Have a nice day!

Some of you may question giving the "glue" by way of the keys back to the customer but it is a calculated risk. It gets back to thinking on your feet and experience with people and human nature. With time, you know when and where to decide on this approach.

Besides, if the customer calls your bluff, there are always backstops. Other faces, other methods. Use this when you're ready. Expand upon the methods and circumstances where this makes sense. Experience breeds 'gut feelings'.

"To thine own self be true."
Quoting fool, ain't I?

14) Curb Close or Door Handle Close.

This could be where the take away close didn't work The customer was a better poker player than you thought!

The Lord "takethed" away on your butt!

There are a great many reasons that a customer is getting ready to take a hike. Bustin' out! They're getting out of Dodge City! Whatever the reason may be, they are either approaching their own vehicle or actually in it and getting ready to exit the paradise otherwise known as your dealership.

This is certainly as good a way to close a deal as others in the right situation. Believe it or not, Mr. Ripley, some customers are experienced enough in their own right that they feel they will not get the best deal until the general sales manager (*very big badge type of dude*) approaches with an offer after all of the underlings have exhausted their efforts. They fight for what they consider the *bottom,* bottom line. They want to feel the desperation of the dealership.

They, like all customers, want to win! Heck, we all do. You know it is a win/win situation. That is not the point. Some like to feel that upper hand. Bragging rights and all that.

That's cool. I will say, though, that the more orchestrated this close is, the more lucrative it may become. There are times when, while still holding gross profit on the deal, the customer could be allowed to walk. Sorry. Wish we could do it. It's just the pure math of the deal. You understand.

The desk folks in the tower are fully aware of the activity, however. Everyone is primed with figures already loaded into that hip bound holster.

As the customer makes his way to leave, the manager is prepared and ready. Being manager, where the deal stands is certainly within grasp. Being manager, he has been there and done that many, many times. Experience!

That is one reason to use this. You are turning the deal while using your teammates. Perhaps, a profit is secured. At the very least, there is a chance for a deal.

In the event there is no way for the manager to make the deal, he knows how to let him out with a chance of making a deal in the future. Not a good thing but it happens. Generally, the customer will be "shot in the foot or leg" with prices that may reflect $300, more or less, below what is thought of as the 'pure, pure' cost. Perhaps this price will sabotage a deal with a competitor and give your dealership a chance to keep the deal together, after all. There is hope that the "back end", known as finance, could make this deal make sense with monies made from their department.

Use the opportunity to make money with this close, though. Sense if the customer seems to be waiting to get through all of the "foreplay" just to make his move to stage left with a final deal waiting. If your timing and gut feelings are right, you could make a paying deal out of a "mini" deal.

15) Assumption Close.

I know: ass'u'me. I saw that demonstrated by Felix on the 'Odd Couple', too. Don't assume. Just as you assumed I would, in fact assume. So you will know, this would have been named differently. As in based on not assuming but knowing! Know this! I know! Don't assume anything!

What would you think of someone suggesting to you, "I am going to 'know close' this deal!"?

"No Close? No way!"

Getting back to that guy who is like 'Denny's': never closes!

So, that is why the "Official Determination Section of Car Close Namers" remained with what is called the *assumption* close. *Know* close was dutifully done away with. *Assumption* close was in!

The salesperson takes for granted this is what will be. There is an attitude with this close that carries over to the customer injecting a feeling of 'business as usual'.

When shopping at Sears, one *assumes* the price on the pair of pants is what will have to be paid at checkout. When the real estate tax bill arrives, one *assumes* it should be paid in full. (Good assumption, that one).

Quite often, when the customer picks up your 'assumptive' attitude, you give evidence why, indeed, it was right to assume. That's the way it is! Done it a hundred times! Taking an order! Done Deal!

You're serving up the numbers. Full pop. All of the pesos. This is what they all do! You buy a toaster with a price tag for $29.99, you pay $29.99 plus tax, if applicable. That is the attitude. Project the feeling that it would be highly out of the ordinary if anything other than what is being presented is proper.

I take my '$29.99 plus tax toaster' to the checkout at Target's and tell the teller, "I'll give you five bucks for this. That would include the sales tax, too!"

Yea, right!

Checkout person pushes a button while yelling, "Security!"

The checkout person has reasonably assumed that any customer wanting that toaster can see the price and is willing to part with that much money to take that toaster home.

Why should buying a car be any different? Okay. You read the history (and 'herstory') section. I am making the point of the attitude, though, similar to the checkout person at a department store. If the people who are a lot smarter and make a lot more money than you for performing the job of setting prices cannot make a determination of a proper price, how can anyone expect you to?

If someone is on your lot looking at cars, why wouldn't you assume they are in the market for a car?

Basic assumptions can be: the customer is driving this car home now; the customer is paying the price on the window; the customer is agreeing to the terms set by the desk manager; you are cute and everybody likes you.

So, maybe assumptions can be wrong. So relate it to being a "business as usual" close.

You may, however, assume that I assume you understand the gist of this close; even if I end up with hooves instead of feet.

16) Free Ticket Close.

Yep. That simple. Oftentimes, dealerships purchase tickets for various trips and events for goodwill as well as that little extra something to finalize a deal.

The customer is done. You know it. There is still just a little bit of 'but' left, though. The customer is rubbing his chin. He's looking to the heavens as if he is really trying to put all that you have offered together.

He's waiting for that little bit of icing on his cake. He is doing you a favor, maybe. Maybe this ticket to Vegas is the only thing that separates this deal from another he was offered.

There are marketing companies who specialize in promotional offers that work on a regular basis with a great many businesses. Even if your dealership is not participating in such a program, offer something on your own; with your dealership's permission, of course.

Free movie tickets; baseball, football, basketball tickets; some type of pass which you feel would appeal to your customers.

As well as a nice gesture, 'closes' with a few freebies thrown in can make all of the difference in closing the deal and are typically one of the more cost effective measures in marketing.

17) Disneyland Close.

It sounds fun already, doesn't it? The Disneyland close. Where are you going now that you have won (the Super Bowl) this fantastic car deal?

Disneyland!

This is a close that gets a means to an end with some buyers. Your anal type with a FICO score in the 700's and higher may not produce the high rate of success as a buyer with perhaps lesser access to cash. Not to say good credit people are anal. Just the anal ones are anal.

The anal ones with poor credit would be tough to do, as well, but for reasons other than just being anal.

Don't confuse this with the anal close. It's not. Also, should any of you happen to be dealing with the author and columnist Carl Hiaasen, remember his books and articles often take pokes at the Disney scheme of things. That would be a reason to refer to this as the *Vacation* close. Since that is what is being offered, that is what it is, after all. 'Disneyland' is so much fun to pronounce, though.

What is being offered is a chance for your buyer to take a vacation. Perhaps there is no opportunity to travel since the buyer feels the purchase is quite enough spending for a while.

But, what if you could give the cash to take a vacation? Three hundred might be enough for some frugal travelers. Maybe five hundred dollars would be the ticket.

Within reason and cooperation of the dealership and lender, oftentimes there is an opportunity to build in enough cash to the finance package that a refund would be in order. I am not speaking of rebates but this is a way to offer a form of "rebate" whether or not one is actually available. It is an honest disclosure since the lender will only approve the deal based on credit and material value, anyway.

Heck, you've discounted the deal so much and giving cash back to take a vacation, too!

To Disneyland, no less!

Just don't ask Car Hiaasen to join you. He's much too busy in Miami writing his next "not pro-Disney" novel.

Also, I do not like 'anal' buyers. I do deal with them, however.

18) The Anal Close.

Censored. The mental picture overwhelms any possibility of use here.

19) Donation Close.

The Humane Society often markets for donations. Calendars are sent with a letter to please donate. Sometimes, they seemingly hit below the belt by sending heart-wrenching photographs of abused and battered pets. The tie of both of the methods is the appeal of allowing the recipient to feel compassion, empathy or pity. Human feeling is being targeted.

To a lesser extent, this approach may be utilized where a deal needs that one more push to get the ultimate "okay".

For instance, where all facets of the deal appear to be in order but perhaps the buyer has the attitude of "well, it all looks good. I just don't know . . . umhhhhhhh. Well, I *maybe* should do it. I just don't know . . . ."

The buyer is right there. Just a little shove is needed.

When you asked the buyer for a driver's license, you noticed a picture in the wallet of a couple of children and a Labrador. Perhaps it was a photo of Fluffy the kitty cat. Maybe you were discussing the merits of owning pets versus the inequities of procreation.

You're dealing with an animal lover.

Perhaps it is any other of a number of causes that could have influence on a buyer: political affiliation, medical research, equal rights causes, children's issues, environmental concerns, and on and on and on . . . .

You have sensed the personality of your buyer at this stage of the deal and have determined hot buttons even outside of the vehicle. Reason: *you are the best! The smartest.*

You also do not qualify for #9 close. Some talent was fortunately scooted right by you.

Action . . . camera . . . you are there with the buyer. Vacillation. Wishy-washy. You have a suggestion coupled with an offer.

Don't know if you could, mind you, but *what if,* along with the deal, we could make a donation to your favorite charity in your name?

Say, $100! (Most likely $75-$80 more than the buyer has ever donated before.)

Well, I don't know about you but I can tell you that there are situations where I would say, "You have a deal!"

It's the bow on the package . . . again.

20) Honor Close.

I know that every person you face you will close. It's a given. I do remember about you being the best there ever was.

However, should your buyer be faced with an emergency at home, lightening struck the dealership and Elvis was spotted shoplifting in your parts department, there could be a time when your customer is leaving without having finished a deal with you. I have heard the rumor through the 'hood that it happens.

Rather than just depend on the "Be Back Bus", get a firm, sincere heartfelt commitment from the customer. Draw on the customer's honor. That is the one and only thing that cannot be taken from an individual. A person has to give honor away when it is lost.

This is what you are banking on. That for a "mere" car deal a customer would not be willing to forego anything other than an honorable transaction and obligation. Even if it is with one you don't suspect of being overly honorable, it may be the last tool available to salvage a deal down the road.

Get an absolute and firm vow that the customer will not purchase from anywhere until speaking with you. You can absolutely and positively guarantee that if they do, they will never know how much more was spent unnecessarily!

Again, this is a case where everyone dealing with you in the dealership has exhausted all means for the moment and there is a legitimate cause for the customer having to leave. Just no time. Sometimes it has to be dealt with.

Follow up immediately with something additional to give the customer hope for gain before he or she even makes it home by leaving a message to the effect of additional values you had overlooked when they were at the dealership. Make it easy for the customer to *be* honorable!

Or you could wait for the "Be Back Bus"!

21) Here Come Da Judge Close.

This has to do with 'your honor'. As in the previous close. Dealing with truly honorable people. Classy people who do not give their word lightly.

I'll preface this with a comment. When I worked in the car business, I found that the better salespeople and managers tended to get even better by setting the bar always higher. They liked the challenges. They appreciated learning. Their egos required that others rely on them and it was a great feeling to have helped when help was needed.

I guess a little of this rubbed off on me. To have the self satisfaction of being a guy people could turn to, I felt I had to earn the right. Regardless of one's accomplishments, today and tomorrow are new days. Yesterday is history. In the car industry, among others, the attitude of "I know what you did for me yesterday but what have you done for me today?" is commonplace.

To get better, one has to think better. Ask for the challenges. That is what some others did and I, as well.

This close developed for me due to a challenge. I would advertise, like others, for others to try to present to me an objection I could not overcome. If successful, I would buy the "winner" lunch or dinner at the restaurant of choice.

I often heard from new salespeople: "what if this . . . ", "what if that . . . ", "suppose a customer said this . . .". I would divide and conquer with my words and the salesperson learned. I learned. We all need the practice.

As confident as I felt, I knew situations could arise where I could be unprepared. I have always felt responsible for the salesperson if I was called into a deal. First and foremost, make the deal! As a matter of pride, I was always willing to take the time necessary to hold the gross profit, as well. My head was never too big but I felt this was my job and my commitment to the salesperson required the best effort the salesperson deserved.

I did, in fact, have to buy a salesman lunch at the Fish Market, a very nice restaurant in downtown Phoenix on Camelback Road.

He had come to me with an objection I could not overcome on the spot. A dilemma. Catch 22. He had experienced the situation and had asked me what could have been done.

I told him, "Don't know! I will know but right now, you've earned a meal on me!"

Frankly, I was more than a little stymied at the time.

Necessity being the mother of invention sans Frank Zappa, I came up with a method of dealing with a seemingly unanswerable objection.

Essentially, the question is how to convince an honorable person to be dishonorable? Yet, have him retain his honor? With your own honor, as well as the dealership's honor, intact?

Solomon, where you be?

The salesman's situation was this: a 'well seasoned' couple had gone through all of the motions of making a car deal. The vehicle was selected, the deal was negotiated to the customers' satisfaction; everything was hunky-dory!

They could not buy the vehicle, though. They *would* not buy. After a manager had attempted all that could be done by isolating objections, there were none. The car was right; the price was right; the dealership was wonderful; the salesman was even better than any they had ever experienced! They had the money needed and the credit required!

On top of all that, they *wanted* to do the deal!

Their immeasurable honor required more: they could not do this deal!

You see, someone had used the previous close with them: the 'Honor Close'. This couple had given their word to a salesman that, regardless of the circumstances, they would not do a deal until they had come back to see him. They shook on it.

So, you see, the honorable customers had no choice. They were wonderful folks that put their pride and honor above all things. All of the world should be made of such folks!

The manager, in trying to make a deal with them, could not emphasize trying to do a deal with our dealership without asking them to go back on their word to the other salesman. To do so would be suggesting the act of lying and being irresponsible could be seen as being acceptable at our dealership.

Sure. The question was asked. Dishonorable people buy and drive, too. One question was enough, though. These folks would certainly not buy from a place of business that expressed its own lack of values by suggesting others not respect their own.

They were properly thanked and let out of the dealership. In following up, our salesman found they had indeed bought the vehicle from the other dealership where the salesman used the 'Honor Close'.

In working to find a suitable solution to the dilemma, I put myself in the 'honorable customers' shoes. I would like to think I, too, value my honor over all. What could a salesperson in this situation present to me that would be neither offensive to my state of honor as well as giving my a good reason to sing praises to all that the deal is done?

An approach I thought would work and satisfied the delicate nature of the situation was put together.

Several months later, I was to put it to the test as I was called into a deal that had the same situation. To think this situation was obscure seemed true since it came up so seldom. I am sure it has happened but I wonder why it never took notice. No solid way to overcome? Lack of honor in people? I don't know but in this case I was fortunate to be prepared.

Same situation with these folks: age, car, money, credit, dealership, salesperson . . . All were wonderful!

They had just made their promise to a salesman at a competing dealership. They intended on honoring it.

Boy, they really wanted to do the deal with us. But you know how it is: a promise is a promise!

I did. I agreed with them. I thanked them accordingly for giving us a shot at doing the deal and suggested the silliness of me trying to extract the same promise from them: I certainly didn't want them to be ping-ponging from dealership to dealership even if they had nothing better to do with their life and overlooked giving an exact and, thusly, "unkeepable" promise!

As we all were about to rise from our seats in the office, a revelation came to me: I asked the couple for the salesman's card. They surely had one, didn't they? (If they hadn't had it I could have gotten it after the fact).

Looking at the business card of the competing salesman, I thought I had heard of him before. I let them know that. Certainly, he was a good and likeable salesman or these folks would not have given their word to him. That fact was a given.

I mentioned we were very discerning about the people we hired at our dealership and could certainly use people such as "Rob Smith", their salesman at the other dealership. Furthermore, I tell how some of our staff who had previously been employed there tell us how fortunate they were to finally make the "big leagues" at our dealership: better pay, better benefits, greater chances for advancement, etc.

"You know," I asked, "if I could get more people of his caliber around here, we would never lack for a prosperous business! Customer service and professionalism compute to success.

"If he had been here today and asked for a position here, would you, as customers, give him a hearty recommendation?"

Of course they would! He was the one who had extracted a promise from them.

"I have an idea. I think this is the answer to all parties concerned. Would you fine people like to save a whole lot of time in addition to money?"

Well, duh . . . I guess!

Having the business card previously I had recorded the number. Mentally or physically writing it down is okay.

I picked up the phone and dialed the number of the other salesman's dealership and asked for him.

I introduced myself (with the couple present) and told him a little of the situation. Of course, I *really* was trying to recruit him, as well. Why not?

I mentioned the better pay cut, benefits, etc. I knew our "mini" deals were better than his dealership's.

I then told them about the deal we had just "made" with "Mr. and Mrs. Mundy" and continued to tell him how impressed they were with him. They had, in fact, "suggested" we look into hiring him.

Since the customers were so willing to back him, I told him I was even *more* impressed! It wasn't ever day that we had customers touting other salespeople so heartily!

As such, I asked where I could send his $100 referral check. (His dealership's "mini" was $75). I wrote the information down, set an appointment to interview him for two days later, thanked him SO much for the referral and placed the phone in its cradle.

Rather a case of acceptance by proxy, wouldn't you say? The couple, overhearing all that was said on my end, were let off of the hook of their honor since the person they gave the promise to allowed a waiver. The other salesman, they heard, had not only accepted the fact that it wasn't any longer necessary to return to his place of business, but they had assisted in helping him out to a chance for a better life. They couldn't have been more proud!

Commitment no longer existing, they continued on with the paperwork and drove their new vehicle on home.

Honor still totally intact.

Money well spent at the Fish Market.

22) Change Shoes Close.

This sounds as stinky as Disneyland sounds like fun! This would probably be the time to point out the advantages of wearing soft-soled shoes in the employment of car sales. Shopping for cars would be easier, as well, with your tootsies more comfortable. Another tip is to never wear your shoes two days in a row so they can always be allowed to dry and prevent fungus. Stinky stuff!

Yes, it would probably be the time to speak of these issues. What would your mother think if you were to suddenly have to go to the hospital with stinky shoes? Have you ever thought just how that could reflect on her maternal efforts in your upbringing? I thought not! Maybe this could be the time to reflect on your duties and obligations to your mom, too. Have a care!

Although this *would* more likely than not be a good time: I suspect you could use some pointers in that area; I won't go there. Instead, let's look to why changing shoes can relate to a close.

The sharper of you have already leaped light years ahead and surmised the caption of number 22 relates to the adage: "Before you judge your neighbor, walk a mile in their shoes." No stink. No Oedipus worries: just the ability to experience empathy and use it to your customer's and your own advantage merely to make that car deal.

Walk a mile in their shoes, so to speak. This is more of an advantage than you first may think. There have been a great many occasions where I have found myself convincing others only after switching my thought patterns to their own point of view. It can give you a perspective as different as front row seats versus the obstructed view section.

When trying to project your own thoughts and opinions on others, it's easy to be thought of as being 'pushy'. Truth be known, that could well be true. In "thinking" with the other party's thought patterns, however, it is surprising how the approach becomes more tactful and certainly can be more convincing.

The key in this approach is to not only switch your shoes but to have your customer slip into yours. In discussing the steps of sales earlier, the customer was invited to assist in the trade evaluation. You allowed the customer to be involved and a sense of teamwork ensues. You are both out to meet and make a common destination. The same sense of psychology is applied in this matter. By showing your ability to relate to and understand the customer's position, another shift can occur with your directness and verbiage.

Your thoughts can revolve around the key point: how can I buy this vehicle? You are now the customer. Right! You think on what you want to hear to make it happen. You are convincing when you relate the reason you are so steadfast in desire to help the customer make the deal.

"If I were in your shoes and trying to buy a car, Mr. Customer, I certainly hope I could depend on your insistence to make this deal. That is the least I would expect! I would want you to sell me! I *want* to hear why it's in my interest to make this happen with you!

"Tell me: if you knew this was a great deal, it was right, it was in the budget, what would you do?

"Would you not give me at least the effort to try to make it happen? For me?

"Would you work as hard for me as I am trying for you?

"Can you deny me working as hard for you as I would hope you would work for me?"

Not pushy, this. Just emphatic. Again, this too, often helps to deal with isolating objections. Unknown walls present themselves to be dealt with.

Attitudes are relaxed. Understanding is absorbed. Both parties are better for the effort.

Good deals are struck.

Now, put your shoes back on your feet." Righty-Tighty Lefty-Loosey" does not apply here. Just put your shoes on the proper feet.

Great job!

23) Think About It Close.

I can hardly imagine any of you out there, whether in sales or life itself, who hasn't been confronted at a time when a decision was really wanted, and I do mean before reincarnation sets in, that a person has come back to you with, "Let me think about it."

I would imagine you have mentioned that a time or two yourself. I think it's to get back at all of the times *you* hated hearing it. Akin to beating the kids because you were beaten.

We do know who you are, too! Being subtle, watch your attitude! It shows!

Just because you were beaten, though, doesn't mean you can't be a little more polite *and* effective in your approach.

Think about it . . . .

As stated earlier, people love to be bolstered by mutual agreement. We like that. Makes us feel smarter! We're accepted. We set the bar by just being us. When people agree with you, don't you feel they are just a little bit smarter? Normally, that's the case. Exceptions exist, but the rule would apply whether it is in negotiations or relationships.

So now . . . You have displayed all of your wares. All of the proper reasons have been demonstrated as to why this is the right purchase. It fits all of the wants, needs, emotional desires and unfulfilled yearnings the customer has ever imagined.

Yet you hear the statement, "I'll think about it."

Or, "Let me sleep on it and I'll get back with you tomorrow."

Or, "I'll talk it over with my wife/husband/significant other tonight. I'll call tomorrow."

Ad nauseum . . . .

Feeling a little spent anyhow, it feels alright just to say alright. Okay to say okay. It is even a little relaxing.

In this close, it really is taking it just a little bit farther, though. Along with agreeing with (and seemingly smarter in the eyes of the client by seeming to agree) the suggestion of "thinking about it" you even show you have a program designed just for folks like them. It is called (trumpets blare now on cue):

THE THINK ABOUT IT PROGRAM!

You have experienced this before. People are making an important decision: perhaps the biggest of their lives. They want to make certain the right move is made. You are not going to change anyone's mind. The point is that most have already made up their mind to buy. You just have to be a salesperson to make it all happen.

You have a program. It is one, which was made for times just like this. You have gone down the list of isolating objections. It is not the price, vehicle, you, the dealership, the monthly payment or rate . . . .

All is in order. The client wants to think about it.

You offer to let them take the vehicle home and give it a try. If all is in order, the deal is done. If not, just let bygones be bygones and let them go along their merry way.

Now, the big disclaimer: DO NOT . . . DO NOT . . . Truly put your client in finance with those conditions if the dealership is not ready to really back it up. If you understand that, let's move on.

The whole point of this is to relax the customer enough to let them avoid all pressure and think about it at the present time.

Get the client comfortable with the alternative of getting a deal that is not binding at this point. There is absolutely no risk. You'd do that, wouldn't you?

Of course. When they appear comfortable with the idea, start with the paperwork.

You may ask, "When you arrive at your home and you and your wife think about it, which part of the deal will be the most important to you? (Isolate objections again . . . if you're a buyer reading this, do the same.) Whether it is tomorrow morning, evening or a month from now, could you be any more informed than what you are at this very moment? You have all you have set out to achieve. The price; the vehicle; the terms. They will not change. I promise. This deal is customized to fit your needs. Folks, the "Think About It Program" is wonderful for those who truly don't know what it is they want. However, it does not come without a cost.

"Let me ask you: if you were waking up with me in your house, and I promise that wouldn't be a pretty sight for you to see, as we were sharing breakfast, would you be excited? Would you feel good? Because I think you will! Not just because you won't have me at the breakfast table but because you have shopped, compared and "thought about" this deal until you know all there is about what is best for you! I can help you but at this point you have helped yourself more than can be imagined!

"If you want to come back to the dealership and wait for finance to get back with you to close the "Think About It" waiver, well then . . . fine. I am suggesting you feel good about what you have already decided and go with it to avoid a return trip and the "Think About It" surcharge. Additionally, I'll get free oil changes to go along with the deal. I'm just thinking of your convenience."

Use whatever is important to the buyer in terms of letting a better deal fall by giving the oil changes, extra gas, another $100 discount, etc. You use your own discretion.

I have used this approach any number of times and it has succeeded more often than not. It is a matter, like all closes, of using when appropriate. Unless stated otherwise, remember all deals are final, though. You're here to turn thinking about it into an action!

Close the deal tightly!

Think about it . . . .

24) Afford It a Year From Now Close.

This close is a play on the Gap close. In our economy, prices of consumer goods typically stay on the rise. No surprise there as a buyer or seller. Where any of us may need an item at the current time or in the near future, it stands to reason to make the purchase of any asset when the cost is minimized. When the item happens to be a depreciating asset, it makes even more sense.

As a seller, you are making the point that it doesn't make economic sense to put off the purchase when the best time to buy is right now! When the buyer feels the vehicle is unaffordable, suggest he returns in a year's time to make the purchase. Assuming the vehicle is, in fact, affordable and the customer has been "carred up" properly, there is no reason not to make the deal.

Continue on to offer the difference in cost out of your own pocket when the buyer does return in a year. Show your commitment to completely satisfy the customer's needs.

Now, if you have allowed enough margin in the deal, you could take a backwards step and make a trip through time itself. Suggest it already *is* a year later. Present the scenario of having the customer a year prior and *now* you're ready to honor the commitment of paying the year's increase in price from last year's model. Make a show of going to the desk manager and "offering to pay" the difference so your customer can take advantage of your deal. Why wait? Prove your sincerity now! If the car's increase was $337.89, show them. Show them next year's model could be twice that amount again!

Have them take advantage of your offer. You may be in the Middle East next year applying these tips to selling Persian carpets.

If a sale doesn't happen, at least you have a customer to follow up with. You'll have to keep reminding that person of your offer to help them get the best deal available.

I am sure the customer would find out that your motto is "buy or die". Not a threat, remember. It's just the biological application of "when the heart stops ticking the Department of Transportation frowns on issuing driver's licenses" to said stopped heart person.

Can't buy a car without a valid license, you know.

25) Service and Parts Department Close.

This is not the truly a close, (this is where someone not so appealing would insert 'if you will'; you know I won't!), but a reinforcement. Along with all of the other positive comments and features of the overall deal, this is putting an emphasis on the complete deal with all the organization has to offer any of its customers.

Dealerships take pride in a variety of areas. Perhaps awards have been issued in Customer Service and/or Satisfaction; perhaps you have the largest in your area, if not the country or world; know if any representatives in Service, Parts or Customer Relations have been singled out for any awards or accomplishments.

Show your own pride in being able to offer such an exclusive opportunity to your buyer. Have them be part of the "team". Mention the advantages due to a "team member" of having a worry-free experience for not only now, but also for the life of the vehicle! Remember to remember: people aren't buying a car; they're buying an existence of having a tool in which to accomplish all of which their lives entail. The less hassle they have in this time of ownership, the better deal there is for them.

This gives you all the more reason to have referrals from them as satisfied customers. Your assurances as such will give a load of confidence to anyone making a buying decision.

Count on it!

26) Contest Close.

You're sure of yourself! Independent! Worldly, wordy and wise! Competitive, even. Daily, you set the bar higher. You want to be the one everyone looks up to. If you do all you hope to do, "hunskies" are hanging out all of your pockets just waiting to be spent on whatever you want. Ben Franklins' feel good to you.

Having reminded you just who you are, any kind of contest is always welcome. Competition is good for the soul. Right up there with chicken soup. Whether you are competing with others or yourself, a sense of winning or the hope of doing just that keeps you fueled up.

We have all been involved in contests where the one who sells the most gets a prize of a trip, favored parking spot, a day off with pay (fat chance in this line of work, I'll tell you.), a gidget, a gadget or a plaque for the wall.

As you are dealing with the customer, there is always the opportunity to have him know you are in such a match. He/she who sells the most gets the trip, etc. It doesn't matter what time of year or month it is: contests hold their own time frames. Ask for help from the customer. I am not saying a customer cares. Maybe that is the case. Just do not count on it. What I am saying is you are in a position and have a reason to offer an even *better* deal than you would normally.

"Mr. And Ms. Customer, I am two cars away from winning the whole kit and caboodle! I have an appointment later on today and it is a done deal, more or less. You are the one I need. I need this deal more than oxygen itself!

"Money-wise, this is huge to me and my family. I need this deal to do it. It is worth money spent by me for your purchase so we can *both* come out ahead! What if I were to put $$$$ of my own money toward the deal? You win, I win, and most importantly, perhaps, my wife/husband wins!"

Use your own discretion as to the amount. If there is an ongoing contest, you'll know how much. If there isn't, create one! Even if the contest is with yourself, you have been nothing but honest throughout the presentation. Your are actually appealing to the customer's self interest but there is also the chance of the customer feeling a little bit of that "giving" feeling that makes most of us feel pretty doggone good.

If you are the salesperson I think you are, you are selling cars, having fun and making money. It makes for more happy customers.

No contest!

27) Alternate Choice Close.

People like to have choices. Not too many, mind you, but two or three to have the plusses and minuses to compare with. Keeping that in mind, it's always a good idea to have the options at your fingertips. This is related to step selling in that you can always move to the lesser-priced vehicle when price continues to be the objection. There is a choice if the customer is trying to convince you that the decision is being made on price, alone. As we've discussed, that is seldom the case. People want bang for their buck. You probably want buck for your bang. No problem, then. Offer the bang the buck is suggesting.

When the vehicle that is really wanted is equipped with a moon roof and price is the stumbling block, fall back to the same model without one. When the four-wheel drive is "too high", fall back to the two-wheeled version. It's really simple, folks. With this much, you get this. With that much, you may get that.

You're justifying your position in relationship to your asking price. The figure you're dealing with is no longer an arbitrary one: it's explained in a newer relationship with something close to what the buyer really wants.

Now, close the deal on the difference of that $2,000 or so in price of the alternate vehicles. People like that choice. Just a small amount for what is really wanted!

28) Negative Close.

When applying any type of close, a little perception by the closer has to be utilized in regard to the potential "closee". If that went without saying, well, I wouldn't have said it. Although there are quite a number of closes to be used in relation to a situation, some will be used a great deal whereas some will seldom, if ever, be used.

You have heard me preach on being positive in dealing with a potential buyer so this is not one that is used nearly as frequently as others. There are those, of course, that may have to be figuratively "slapped" just to get a little attention. I am not saying to "take away your client's face". One should always be allowed to save said face. Just know when the time is present to get your potential buyer's attention.

For instance, a buyer may be reluctant to give any indication of taking you up on your offer and is perhaps a little rude and obnoxious in the approach to you. Other closes have apparently been ineffective. You want to give notice that, although negotiations haven't expired, they may be drawing near.

You may want to say, "Mr. Ruth, I think I do understand. This offer and vehicle do not appeal to everyone.

"Perhaps, you may want to consider a much lesser vehicle. Could I give you a referral to one of our competitors?"

Again, this is an example. It is a little negative. You may be "without Ruth": literally and figuratively. You may or may not make a deal. You can make your customer stand up and take notice, however.

Reading between the lines, this may be the time for a new "face" to save the deal. That is for you to know as the standing on his feet kind of thinker, though.

Besides, there is always the "curb close".

That would be number 14 in this section, kiddos.

29) Lost Sale Close.

This close is merely an approach to making the deal when all seems to be right but the customer is reluctant, yet again, to commit. A variable of "isolating objections", questions and statements are directed to ask of the customer where perhaps the deal went wrong. You're asking questions (nothing new, right?) of the customer to, from the customer's perspective, improve your selling skills in the future.

Simply, you want to inquire where you went wrong in your approach. "Was it this?" "Was it that?"

Finding where you made an error, perhaps in judgment, approach or presentation will help you in the customer's brethren of the future. Of course, the point of the exercise is to isolate the objection in *this* deal and then to overcome it.

With the appropriate "thank you's", then close the deal.

30) Referral Close.

One of many ways of appealing to the practicality and "hope for gain" of the buyer, the "Referral Close" can be utilized in any number of ways. The point of this close is to not only make a deal but to "farm" for future potential customers.

This is hardly a new concept. The practice of 'Quid pro Quo' has been around since the beginning of time. "I'll do for you if you do for me." "If you do this, I will do that."

This is a close to be used as a sort of dressing: you feel the deal about to be signed, sealed and delivered and this is just one more extra you really want to share with your customer. A typical application would be to offer to help make the first payment of the new vehicle your customer is about to buy if any of the customer's friends, family or co-workers were to come in to see you and purchase a vehicle themselves.

A form of a "Bird Dog", this approach is tied directly to the monthly payments to show just how easy this deal can be consummated. Furthermore, it could go on indefinitely should the buyer have enough acquaintances and drive to continue to send you clients.

An approach that has been practiced with great success is to offer $100 toward the first payment with the first referred customer. With a second referred customer, $200 additional is applied. With a third and any future customers in the year, $300 is promised and delivered.

In the average car payment, the amount of $300 could go a long way toward making the bulk of the payment virtually go away. With a positive approach, most people will look at the difference as the "real" payment. For example, should the payment be $430 a month, the "real" payment would merely be $130 with only one referral a month after the initial two referrals. This really works!

Remember to remember, money does make money! Spend it properly and it comes back to you multiplied.

Be advised, to make sure you are not working "mini deals", let the desk know when you are working the referrals that the "Bird Dog" is included in the deal. This is no deterrent as you've found referrals are the best customers of all. Someone known and trusted has recommended you thus you offer assurances of having already passing the test of being a certified professional and trustworthy in your own right.

With proper record keeping, good follow up and a drive to succeed, this is one of the better ways to expand your "private enterprise".

31) Intimidation Close.

This close is a somewhat subtle approach to the 'Negative Close' in that you're putting a buyer on the spot but not openly trying to be aggressive toward him. Ideally, when dealing with two or more customers at a time, you want for everyone to be on the same page. Being in agreement is always the most amicable setting to be involved in—without question. There are times, however, when one senses the opportunity to have one customer nudge the other into conformance. You can just feel the wife fantasizing of a life with the new mini van. You see the dreamy look in the husband's eyes when he is imagining the hunting and fishing expeditions in his new 4X4. Or perhaps, being politically correct again, the situation is reversed. Alrighty and cool . . . .

You feel that whatever perceived objection the hesitating party has can be overcome by merely acting to please his or hers life's partner. Don't we all want to be given thanks for being giving and unselfish? Don't we all sometimes like to feel owed by someone who would pay in return?

You could approach this scenario with a set of questions such as: "When you first married your wife/husband, wouldn't you have bought her/him two of these vehicles? Don't you at least love her/him half as much now?"

Or, state the obvious: "Perhaps this isn't the vehicle that you wish and dream for but isn't your wife's/husband's dream more important to you?"

Properly presented, the intimidation is not being rendered by you but rather by the partner. It's up to you to know when and where to take this "tactful" approach.

Just sit back and enjoy while you roll into your assumption close and start with the paperwork.

32) Power of Suggestion Close.

Have you ever had a song in your head that just wouldn't go away? Surely, you have. Those of you experienced in taking the ride through one of Disney's attractions would testify that "It's a Small, Small World" is an example of a song that really sticks with you. Sing along, now.

"It's a small . . . small . . . world . . . ."

You have had a suggestion and, at least for a few moments, the prompting of it caught you rehashing a song you may want to relish, or not.

Communication is a wonderful thing. That is what all of this writing has been about. Politicians use the power of suggestion on a regular basis. It still makes us ponder the deep and philosophical statement: "I depends upon just what the definition of 'is', is."

Regardless of how many of you will consider that to perhaps be an inane statement, it does make us think about it. It was spoken by one of the consummate salesmen of our lifetimes.

If you know who it is, consider yourself brilliant and strike up a cigar!

Now, whenever we want something, we bring it up in a positive light whether it is to ourselves or to whom we depend upon to get it. Someone may want the new kitchen: "But Darling, it will make our home so much more appealing. The cost will be made up when we sell the home."

Maybe someone wants a new RV: "Honey, we will never be without a room while we're traveling on the road. And, just think: we won't be spending a lot of dough on a bunch of hotels and motels. You'll love it!"

Justification, ain't it?

Well, that is exactly what you're about to do in this close. Justify your suggestion. The seed is planted, cultivated and harvested.

The customer may be considering why the purchase should be made now instead of later. It is your job to let the customer *know* why!

It is the 'Power of Suggestion'.

For example, "Folks, I guess I know you're shopping now since you know when you buy off-season the best deals are around. Did you know that shopping on Tuesday (Wednesday, Thursday, Sunday, etc.) you can get an even *better* deal?"

Or: "Incentives will never be as good as this for a long, long time: if *ever*!"

Perhaps: "Buying right before Christmas is the best time. It's a little known insider tidbit!"

Maybe: "The first part of the year is the best time to buy! The manufacturer and dealership like to get out to a big lead over all of the competition!"

There is no twisting of the truth since the truth is you want the sale badly. Your dealership wants the deal badly. The manufacturer wants the deal badly.

The customer wants the deal badly.

So, plant the seed that makes the 'Power of Suggestion' do its job. We're all in this together, right? "It's a small . . . small . . . world . . . ."

33) 'Hidden' or 'Sharp Angle' Close.

Here is a revelation: there are shoppers who come onto the lot during off hours and check your inventory!

Have you ever dealt with one of them? They have found the vehicle they are looking for in a remote corner and depend on your not having the knowledge of it being in stock. Perhaps they merely drove through the lot and didn't see it where they expected to see it and figure they can work a deal and not obligate to buying it since it is not there. It also creates pressure on the salesperson to discount a vehicle nearly like the one the shopper presumably wants.

They obviously have never dealt with you, the consummate professional! You *have* walked the lot. You *have* checked out the PDI (preparation, delivery and inspection) area! You *have* knowledge of what vehicles are incoming from the rails or car hauler!

And they thought they were going to get one over on you. Shame on them! You are *sharp*! You are *informed*! You *know* about the *hidden* assets, aka vehicles!

The customer may suggest to you that a purchase could be forthcoming: if only you had the vehicle wanted! "Sigh . . . ."

Following the customer's cue, work the deal as if there is no vehicle at the moment in stock. Ask for the options and equipment you *know* is offered on the particular vehicle that is desired.

Then: "What if?"

"What if we could make you a deal on that vehicle? You said 'if only it were in stock'. If we had it, would you do the deal *right now!*"

Of course, the buyer may be a little curious. Overall, he will most likely be confident in your inability to supply the vehicle 'right now'. So, you move on with the deal.

Pleasantly, at the moment chosen by you to be the most effective, your "runner" has just returned to you with the wonderful news that the dealership, does, in fact, have the exact vehicle you need! Wow! Who knew?

Hopefully, perhaps predictably, write up the deal.

34) Demonstration Close.

Product knowledge and experience with the marketplace is paramount here. There are always buyers who have a brand loyalty and may be going through the motions to satisfy a partner or perhaps their own curiosity. The "Poopfire" is faster than the "Belchfire". The "Poopfire" is safer than the "Belchfire".

Your mission, should you decide to accept it, is to point out the correct facts the shopper has pointed out to you but to show a few facts of your own the shopper is perhaps not acquainted with.

An example of agreeing but contradicting would be to point out the fact of the "Poopfire's" top speed is, in fact, 3 miles per hour faster than the "Belchfire's" but maybe that wouldn't be as important since there would probably never be a time that the car would be "red-lined" to that point. "However, Mr. And Ms. Shopper, did you know that, due to higher torque, the "Belchfire" is 1.5 seconds faster in getting from 0 to 60 miles per hour! Isn't merging onto the interstate and having less exposure in the passing lane more important to you than what *could* be?

Maybe you could demonstrate the higher resale value of your product. 'Mayhaps' there are options included at no additional cost which the shopper's favorite doesn't offer.

"Keep your friends close but keep your enemies closer."

Apply that well-known adage to your competition. Know what the "Poopfire" line has to offer, both good and bad. With your knowledge, you are able to frame your approach to virtually any situation a shopper has to offer.

All you have to do is demonstrate what your product and you will do to better the shopper's advantage by dealing with you and *your* product.

Going further in instances, take the customer to the vehicle yet again and re-demonstrate the points of interest of the greatest importance. Have the vehicle test driven again if that is what it will take! Remember, with acceptance of this further demonstration the customer is showing a willingness to buy.

Demonstrate your sales ability and let the customer do just that!

35) Summary Close.

This close is precisely what it insinuates. A summarization is given of key points you know is important to the buyer. Relate the points as you know them from the first contact with the buyer. Not unlike a trial attorney, you are pulling up facts that will influence an ultimate decision. You are, indeed, appealing to a jury.

Keep the items in their pecking order and re-emphasize the fact that all have been addressed. The budget is in line; the safety of the vehicle is more than the customer had realized; the gas mileage and overall economy are well within the expectations; warranties are more than satisfactory; the trade allowance was great . . . etc.

Not to mention just how wonderful you happen to be! Strikingly attractive, to boot!

You are closing in on the finish line with an uplifting and positive note. Any negatives the customer may be artificially harboring are thrown by the wayside. It is truly a wonderful life!

Golly gee whiz, you are truly the BEST!

36) The Three Demons Close.

As stated previously, closes are merely an application of common sense and purpose. They come from a myriad of sources: all relate back to experience.

Some basic closes are taught in training classes and seminars while others are passed down from one to others while "smokin' and joking" in the lounge or outside "rest" area.

Be advised smokin' is politically incorrect. Joking has yet to be judged as a whole.

Some closes are quick to present and to be realized. Others are stretched a bit and even carried from one closer to another. This close represents an anecdotal type of close where you perceive your customer to be somewhat patient, yet perhaps, indecisive.

This relates again to the person who wants to ponder the deal; options have to be weighed; the weather has to be forecasted.

In short, the customer wishes to "think about it".

Because this is not an infrequent occurrence, I refer again to this objection. This is yet another way to address the wishy-washy of the public.

This close is presented as a joke or even as a short story. You're building a "log cabin" as I have been accused of doing in the past. That is fine and dandy. Just close the deal and make it a good one.

Ask the customer if he has ever heard of the "Three Demons and Mephistopheles". The Devil, Beelzebub, Horned Dude or your Mother-in-Law may be substituted in place of the long 'M' word if so inclined.

For the record, I really adore my Mother-in-Law. (She may proof read this, too.)

Continuing, you tell the story of how the nasty guy down under is interested in increasing his recruits to the Netherworld and summons his three best recruiters. He raises his "home place" and screams at Duh Demon, the first recruiter to step forward.

"I want more souls! How will you get them for me?"

Duh Demon replies, "I can get you half of all that are on earth, your 'Meanliness'. I suggest I go to the mortal world and disguise myself as a human, spreading the word that there is no God, no Devil, no Heaven and no Hell. They can do anything their little hearts desire with no fear of retribution! I guarantee half the people will believe, run amuck and hit the highway straight to your domain!"

The Big Guy liked that!

Dingo Demon, not to be upstaged, stepped forward. "I can do even better, oh Glowing One! I can get three fourths of the souls to you. I, too, would go to the mortal world disguised as a mortal and tell them there is, indeed, a God, a Devil, Heaven and Hell. I would insist they go to their respective houses of worship once a week. On the other six days, however, all were free to do any and everything their corrupted hearts desire. On the day of worship, they only have to ask for forgiveness and all their transgressions will be forgiven. (Oh, I do *love* to lie!)

"We will have to widen our entrances to admit so many of the droves that will be heading our way!"

Dagger, the meanest demon of them all, shoved Dingo aside. "I'll get you each and every soul, Dude!" Being Mephistopheles' favorite, Dagger could slide a little on minor transgressions.

"Dingo and Duh did, at least, get one idea right. That is, go to the mortal world as one of them. The difference is in the harvesting. I will get ALL of the souls to be had!"

The Big Guy, momentarily taken back with the 'Dude' address, smiled at this suggestion from his favorite demon.

Dagger stared into his fiery eyes and continued. "After I spread the word, you will grin horn to horn! The word will be that all exists: Heaven, Hell; Good and Evil; God, and of course, your Horniness."

(Dagger came back to his mentor with a sign of respect.)

"I'll give them the Truth. I will tell them if they don't do as their 'Good Books' say, they will take the highway straight to Hell, good intentions be damned. I will tell them their souls will be yours forever. I will let them know what they will suffer through all eternity. But . . . throughout their mortal lives they may have anything and do anything their insignificant hearts desire."

"I will add an allowance: all of the people may take all of the time they want to "think about it".

Cute, huh. An off hand way of saying "thinking about it" will land you straight in Hell.

Perhaps you'll get a chuckle or two. Unless you're Robin Williams, that won't matter. Since now you will look your buyer in the eye and say, "Let's do the deal."

Thinking is over. Action will take you straight to the "Promised Land".

CHAPTER 9

LEASING AUTOMOBILES

Leasing is a concept of financing that has opened new avenues for auto manufacturers and dealers to sell to the public. Even though it has been around for decades, there are those among us who are still a bit skeptical about "buying" a lease. In my view, part of the misconception of leasing is in confusing the idea with rental cars-we have all heard of Avis, Hertz, Alamo and others. These are 'rental' companies. Their product allows consumers to use a vehicle for a limited time for an agreed amount. Leasing a vehicle also allows consumers to use a vehicle for a contracted time. Perhaps that is as far as the uninformed care to explore the idea.

First, long live the car rental companies. We all have a time when we have need of a vehicle for a short period of time: when we travel to locations far from home, when our own vehicle is in the shop for repairs or when a larger capacity vehicle is required to transport more passengers than is the norm in your life. Maybe you want to rent a vehicle to check out the various models available to make a better buying decision. There are a lot of reasons to "rent".

So, lets get to a little bit of information about what leasing is. After reading this, you make your own decisions and opinions.

Acquiring an automobile involves the exchange of goods. We have covered that. It's a no brainer. If one is purchasing a vehicle, financing is normally involved. There are those who pay cash in full but they are in the small percentage of the equation.

So, outside of those who pay cash on the barrelhead for their car, who owns the vehicle? For those of you who continue to toss out the words "I want to own my car", take notice: the lender has a lien against your vehicle! Therefore, by laws of our wonderful land, the lender owns your vehicle until you have satisfied your contractual obligations. If in doubt, pay only 71 payments of your 72 required and wait to see if some very unpleasant action doesn't occur. The bank *will* do what is necessary to either get their final payment, with fees and penalties, and/or the vehicle itself. Yet, some continue to think they are the legal owners. Interesting.

Now, if 35 payments were made on a 36-month lease and the owner ignored the final payment, similar actions would occur. This isn't a matter of leasing versus buying: it's a matter of people keeping their agreements. In both cases, money was lent to a party for the purpose of having a vehicle that could be named "Hot Stuff" or "Matilda". Vanity plates could be purchased in either case.

Similarities exist between installment buying and leasing. Both require vehicle registration; both require vehicle insurance; both require money to be paid to the lender at a pre-determined time.

Accepting the fact that the vehicle is not owned by the daily user in either leasing or 'buying on time', it becomes an issue other than the "I want to own my car" stated objection. Becoming an owner of a bank note (purchasing) or an owner of a lease note are the two "ownership" issues.

What should be of most value in considering which would be the most beneficial to the 'buyer' is in what manner will the vehicle be used? In the initial fact gathering, the following questions should be answered:

1) How long does the buyer typically keep his/her vehicle?
2) How many miles per year are driven?
3) Are keeping up with the newest safety and performance standards important issues?
4) Overall, does the idea of avoiding major overhauls to the vehicle appeal to the buyer's sense of values?
5) Back to the old I.Q. question: Does the buyer want to pay more . . . or less?

    a. Would the buyer want more car for less money? (Or)
    b. Less car for more money?

(Leasing laws may differ from state to state so make certain you are up to date on how those regulations apply in your neck of the woods. Here, I am speaking with respect to how leasing exists in the state of Arizona.)

The concept of leasing is a rather simple one: you pay the lender for the anticipated depreciation of the vehicle plus interest. It is that easy to explain. It is that basic of an idea.

Let's take two vehicles, Car 1 and Car 2, which are identical in every way other than financing. Car 1 is leased while Car 2 is being paid for in purchase installments. Car 1 is being leased for three years. Car 2 is being financed for five years.

At the time of purchase the price of the car was $25,000. This applies to both cases, as well. It is still the same car. No money down is used here. (For you engineering finance dudes, I am skimming over the basics: don't pick on my figures!)

In a purchase deal, no thought is given to what the value of the car will be in three years. What will be, will be.

In this example, the value after three years, known as the 'residual', will be $15,000 for leasing purposes on Car1.

So, Car 2 is being purchased for $25,000, plus fees, plus registration, plus tax on the entire amount of the purchase. If a trade is involved, tax is applied to the difference of the price. We don't have a trade. The car was totaled that may have been traded. We're keeping it simple here: KISS.—

Let's figure out some numbers:

Selling Price:	$25,000
Fees	495
Registration	525 (Arizona is a little steep!)
Sales Tax (8.1%)	2,025
Total	$27,520
Payment—60m. @ 7%	$544.93
Total of payments:	$32,695.80

For 60 payments of $544.93, the buyer of the vehicle will ultimately own a five-year old vehicle. Until then, the lender will have first legal rights to it. Again, when the vehicle is finally owned, it is older, more expensive to maintain, already has a second set of tires and is impatient to try out its third set and it has cost over $32,000 in payments plus additional maintenance to get there. It has 60,000 miles on the odometer and the buyer could be tired of it.

Couldn't wait to *really* own it just so it could be traded in: free and clear.

Who knew?

Car 1 still had the fees. It had the registration. It, too, had tax. The difference is the tax was applied to the payment rather than the to the total cost of the vehicle. Typically, the first payment will be paid at the time of the deal and the tax applied appropriately.

Let's figure out the car 1 numbers:

Purchase Price		
(for leasing figures)	$25,000	
Residual (55%)	13,750	
Depreciation	$11,250	(Difference of purchase: less future value)
Fees	495	
Registration	525	
Tax (on 1st pmt.)	30.	

I am not going into the explanation of money factors and the financing of the lease. Go to "Lease School" for that training. I want to show the amount of cash out of pocket for the same vehicle, same use and same trips to the home, vacation and work.

So add up the depreciation, fees, registration and tax. Interest is applied to both the residualized portion of the vehicle as well as to the depreciation. Interest and the amount financed are taken into account as in any loan and the payment would be, in this case, around $367 per month plus tax of $30 per month. The monthly payment would then be $397.

Car 1 costs:
(Pmt. X 36) $14,292

Car 2 costs:
(Pmt. X 36) $19,617

Over the same three years, Car 2 cost over $5,000 more. Why? It's more to finance and more commitment.

Car 1 "owner" may now drop off the keys to his car. Good thing, too! Tires will soon be needed.

Car 2 "owner" needs another tune-up and needs to budget for tires and shocks. Bet he can't wait to make the next payment on a car going on four years old.

Another thing should be mentioned: the Car 1 lease deal is a Closed End Lease. It allows the 'owner' to buy the vehicle at the end of the lease term. Three years before, when estimating the residual, or future value, the manufacturer set the price at $13,750. If the value is significantly less than that estimation, chances are the buyer would not exercise the purchase option and merely turn the car back in. This would be an I.Q. test again. However, (based on the local or "book" values) should the value be higher than the residual owed the lender, the buyer has the option to buy the car outright or trade it in on the next deal. Be aware sales tax would be owed on the selling price at that time should the car be purchased. What a great deal! The lender takes the risks while the buyer reaps the low-risk benefits!

Buyer of Car 1 lease also realized a lesson when the previous car was totaled: although the car was only bought three months prior, a sales tax of $1,800 was included in the financing. He realized the state had a poor record of refunding pro-rated sales taxes on wrecked cars. Imagine!

Buyer of Car 2 didn't think of that. He instead paid the first $1,800 that is gone forever and paid an additional $2,025 to create a new base for which new interest could be applied.

A 'Closed-End Lease' is one in which the lender is responsible for the future value; not the buyer. An 'open-end lease' puts the responsibility on the buyer. If your state has not outlawed open-end leases in your area, don't agree to one unless suitable duress had been applied-like if your teeth are being yanked out without the anesthesia.

Typically, today's leases also come with what is known as 'Gap' insurance. Should your car be totaled or stolen, Gap insurance kicks in to help make up the difference owed to the bank between your insurance coverage and what is owed, when applicable. In recent years, installment loans on purchases have been known to supply 'Gap' insurance, as well. One may have to ask about it, however.

To summarize, the same vehicle may be had for less money, there are more options with less obligations and sales tax is applied to only the amount of the vehicle you actually use.

So . . . what's the catch?

The so-called 'catch' is that the better leases are available only to "well qualified" buyers, to use the advertisers label. Credit ratings of the buyer have to be somewhat excellent: Fair Isaac Scores have to be in the 600's or higher. The lenders are marketing leases to those who have shown clues indicating more responsibility in their overall lives. That is not to say that those with lower scores are necessarily irresponsible; it's just that those people wouldn't qualify for a lease. One response I have given when asked why one should lease is: 'Because you can'. It really is an opportunity to prove the old adage: "The rich get richer while the poor get poorer."

Not all who have great credit are rich but they sure will help themselves by getting less poor.

There are circumstances, of course, which would make leasing less appealing. If a person drives over 20,000 miles per year, leasing would probably not be to the buyer's advantage. Up to that mileage, it is certainly looking in to.

Common leases would include mileage of 10,000, 12,000 or 15,000 per year. It depends on the lender, make of the vehicle and term of the lease. After the allowed mileage, additional miles may be purchased for around ten cents to fifteen cents per mile. If your normal driving was 3,000 miles per year over the allowance, an additional $300 to $450 per year could be pro-rated into your lease contract and your payments would reflect the added cost accordingly.

Remember, car 1 and car 2 being the same vehicle, will have the same depreciation whether it's leased or purchased. The adjustments for mileage are made by the 'book' at roughly the same cost as leasing. Added mileage over an acceptable 10,000 to 12,000 miles per year will lessen the value of the vehicle. Since leasing lenders don't want "ragged out" vehicles at lease end, the limits are set as to just how many miles are allowed but still have similar mileage depreciation figures as the 'book'. My figure of 20,000 miles is number I have found to be at its maximum and usually the figure would be around 18,000 miles per year where buyers could benefit from leasing.

Insurance required on leased vehicles is typically a more comprehensive policy with 100/300/50 thousand coverage. The premium is higher than the minimums otherwise set but those with credit will, for the most part, have more assets in their lives and would do well to have the same coverage even if it were on a purchase. The more you have, the more you may lose. Cover your butt!

(The preceding was brought to you by those folks who objected to a lease: basing said objections on their increased premiums. Without them, I may not have bothered mentioning it at all.)

Now that we have determined proper insurance coverage for you and your associates, we will return to reasons to lease or not to lease: that is the question.

For buyers who have told you their past ownership periods were for longer periods, such as five to ten years or more, determine if that practice still holds. It may or it may not. People's habits change and are sometimes influenced by others. We have our own opinions about how we practice ownership and buying practices and change only when there is a beneficial reason to do just that.

I have am opinion for my lifestyle like everyone else. I subscribe to the belief that if you want a new car: lease. If you want to purchase: buy a used vehicle that is one, two or three years old with its major rate of depreciation already behind it and perhaps still has some factory warranty remaining. That's just me. With persuasion, I could be influenced under the right circumstances to change my mind. I might just ask to be sold on the idea with the salesperson giving me a reason to keep my mind open to his or her ideas.

There are other advantages to leasing that could save you additional funds come trade-in time. Should your vehicle be involved in an accident, whether purchased or leased you would have repairs made by an authorized body shop. Accepting the work was done in a highly professional manner, chances are that when trading in your 'purchased' vehicle the owner would take a significant 'hit' in trade-in value: sometimes thousands in losses! When turning in the leased vehicle, inspections are made to determine 'wear and tear' but the accident history will not require any additional fees to be paid. Exceptions exist but the rule applies more often than not.

In a nutshell, leasing is sometimes referred to as a 'Gas and Go' program since gas and oil are about the only things necessary to spend hard earned money on. Normal maintenance is required, of course, but in no different a fashion than recommended for a vehicle no matter how it is financed.

Presenting simple financial advantages to your buyer could have a loyal and devoted customer for years to come. Additionally, you're aware when the lease will be coming to fruition and can be helpful in your customer's decision-making process.

Showing the advantage of saving even $100 per month by using a leasing program versus an installment loan over a period of years can be quite impressive. Consider a twenty-year span of saving $100 per month. That is 240 months at $100 equals $24,000 in savings! For the same vehicle and that figure doesn't even take into account the money saved on repairs, maintenance, tires, etc.

Imagine what an investment of $24,000 over twenty years could come to. If invested in an average bond, the amount could be $40,000 or more.

As stated: the rich get richer!

CHAPTER 10

CLOSING SUMMARY

Three dozen closes have been listed with some 'pros' and 'cons' of leasing following up. Of these, there are a few that will be used with regularity since the *reasons* to use them are quite obvious and occur with virtually every transaction. As to the remaining, they are perhaps best referred to as "specialty" closes where the circumstances may not present themselves often but when they do there will be a way to address the situation.

As a seller of goods, it is your responsibility to use everything at your disposal to make a deal. The buyer, experienced or otherwise, expects that from the sales person at the very least. As a buyer, you expect it in return. If you have a lick of sense, you will realize when the tables are turned with you in a buying situation. As a more informed sales professional, you will appreciate the various methods used to enlighten you when you have some personal difficulty in making a buying decision. Being in an informed and educated position as a *professional* not only makes your job smoother but allows the buyer to, maybe, just maybe, have a really enjoyable time while doing business with your and your dealership.

The paragraph above swings a little back and forth between wearing buying or selling shoes. That is intentional. It's just a hair confusing simply because that, my informed friends, is the point. The fine line between buying and selling is *very* fine! Again, knowing how to buy means you know how to sell.

So, you know how to sell, huh? Do you personally get the shakes when *you* go to buy a car? When you accompany a friend or family member to help him or her make a deal?

Yea, right! I would bet you're totally shaken at the very prospect. See? You delight in the opportunity to go out and buy a car yourself. There are no "Boogie Men" to intimidate you. You know your life is such that when you go to personally shop for any item there are guidelines you wish to follow and you expect the sales professional you happen to be dealing with to help you follow those guidelines.

It's their job. You appreciate that fact. You come to realize if all had some experience in these types of sales all of our jobs would be simpler; by far.

You may think of objections to doing a deal yourself. So then, why are you there in a buying position? You may be waiting to meet a salesperson to allow you the fun of exchanging something for something else. Furthermore, any closes presented to you would be overwhelmingly welcome! It helps you follow the route you wanted to take. You know the closes are based on common sense and like it or not, sometimes it applies to you, too.

Quite frankly, there are times when things could be speeded up by presenting the uninformed with a list of these closes. In understanding, all could realize there is no smoke with mirrors; there is no misdirection; there is a good and old fashioned meeting of mutual wants and needs.

Closing with understanding is thrown in for no charge.

Twenty Goals as a Professional Salesperson

1) Have knowledge of product with proper demonstration skills.
2) Build value in you, your dealership as well as your product.
3) Do a proper trade evaluation when applicable.
4) Know your stock.
5) Show enthusiasm throughout your day. It carries over to your customers and co-workers.
6) Be informed of potential sources of down payments. Creativity *may* make the deal!
7) Learn to be a good negotiator.
8) Know how to follow direction. It helps when you are the leader.

9) Use proper attire. Your appearance means a great deal!

10) Be diligent in your pursuit of success.

11) Don't forget the basics! Leave the short cuts to those who will self-destruct!

12) Learn how to serve up the numbers in the deal. Presentation is everything!

13) Communicate: with your customers, management, co-workers as well as yourself!

14) Learn how to properly T.O. (Turn Over) a customer to management.

15) Always believe in the deal. It's there!

16) Know your competition.

17) Have at least a basic concept of financing options: purchases and leases.

18) Understand the importance of making and keeping appointments.

19) Work referrals!

20) FOCUS! Focus on everything above and the goals you have set for you, your family and life, itself.

So: What's Your Thinking?

You've been overloaded with all of this information regarding on how to "buy" a car. That is, in knowing how to "sell" a car, or anything, for that matter, buying is a walk in the park. For those of you that were 'merely' into self-improvement, I see easier trails through the generations of vehicles you will purchase down the road. Pun intended.

For you dudettes and dudes who are seriously looking for a career, is it to be doctor, lawyer, "Native-American" (I AM a p.c. type of dude!) chief?

Consider George Carlin's remark on various occupations:

"If lawyers are disbarred and clergymen defrocked, doesn't it follow that electricians can be 'delighted', musicians 'denoted', cowboys 'deranged', models 'deposed', tree surgeons 'debarked', and dry cleaners 'depressed'?"

Certainly, there can be pitfalls to any occupation. I don't know about you, but I surely would hate to be 'debarked'! Being thick skinned and all, you know.

Following the same line of thought as ol' George there, I guess you would "dis-carred" the bad car salesperson. A stretch, I know, but it's as close as my neuron-starved brain would allow.

Discarding my poor taste in attempted humor, I will give you the definition of career as given by "The New Lexicon Webster's Dictionary of the English Language":

"Career (kerier) 1. n. a swift movement, impetus, *the horse's headlong career* // progress through life with respect to one's work / / a means of earning a living, a profession (also used attributively, *a career diplomat*) in full career at top speed 2. *v.i.* to move swiftly and erratically (F. *carriere,* race course)"

Curiously, Webster's uses one of our oldest modes of transportation as an example to define how one would pursue a professional life: the horse. Stemming from the French word 'carriere', I would imagine our influential ancestors felt life was merely a course to be run in circles. Running at full steam ahead, I might add. Similar to the Celtic I spoke of in the beginning. Different source of info.

With the recent overwhelming popularity of NASCAR, future editions of the dictionary may well choose to use the automobile on its respective track as an example: *the auto's headlong career//.* Who knows?

At the start of this writing, I mentioned a little of the background due to transportation and the automobile. There have been many fortunes won, lost and yet won again in the dealings associated with the manufacturing, promotions and sales of the product. We have been in this cycle for over a century. I would imagine, regardless of improvements, technology advancements or applications we will continue to depend upon what has become an integral segment of our daily lives.

So, consider whether or not you desire to be part of where we have yet to explore. The pay and satisfaction could well be worth all you could possibly imagine!

For those of you who read this far in spite of having no interest in the career aspect and just wanted to know how to buy a car, enjoy the view as well as the new and easier process. The car salesperson *always* welcomes an informed buyer.

For both groups: regards from 'Org and Tumba' and *"Enjoy the ride!"*

Roc Leatherbury